Futures and Frosting

A SUGARCOATED
HAPPILY EVER AFTER

BY TARA SIVEC

For my husband. Thanks for always reading what I write and for not giving me a hard time when I demand that you tell me if it's shit or not. Thanks for not telling me anything I make you read is shit. Thanks for giving me your honest opinion on yeast infections and not throwing up on me.

For Buffy – my sister from another mister and my honest-to-God soul mate. "Slut – did you mean to say Buffy?" Someday we will live in the same state and the world will explode from awesomeness. Fact

For my family. You are all bat shit crazy but I wouldn't have it any other way. Thank you for tee time, ceiling fan baseball and "can you smell that?" Without you, my life would be extremely boring.

CONTENTS

ACKNOWLEDGEMENTS

There are so many amazing people I need to thank that I could probably fill up an entire book with just their names.

First and foremost – my amazing editor Max. You are the wind beneath my skirt and I love you! Thank you for all of your help and support. I will hump your leg for days when we're in the same room together.

Colleen Hoover - I can never thank you enough for the support you have given me. You never hesitate to answer my gazillion questions and you give me hope that someday I will be as awesome as you! I'm so happy for you and all of your success!

Sarah Hansen – you are the twin I never knew I had. Thank you for always supporting me, making me laugh and putting up with my husband's Facebook posts. Jason Voorhies is still a pussy.

Mollie Harper – I adore you! And not just for the Floppy Vag song or the amazing "Pay it Forward" movement. Okay, those might be the main reasons, I'm not gonna lie. You are amazing and sweet and you put a smile on my face constantly.

To my Slappers – You were my first supporters and fans in this crazy endeavor and I will be forever grateful that I met all of you. I love you from the bottom of my heart.

To all the hookers at Bookaholics Anonymous and Book Broads – I love you. Each and every one of you. I'm so glad I "met" you. You are amazing and your support is never-ending. Thank you so much for all of the "Pay-it-Forwards", pimping and just general awesomeness.

7

To all of the other Indie authors out there – I am proud and humbled to be in the same circle as you. I hope everyone realizes just how hard you work on a daily basis to make your dreams come true.

And last but not least, thank you SO much to the following blogs who reviewed/featured my book(s) on their pages. If I skipped someone, I'm so sorry. It's all Google's fault:

Aestas Book Blog, Ana's Attic, Ashley's Book Nook, Book Liaison, Book-Snobs, Coffee, Books and Lipgloss, Confessions of Novel Junkies, Cursed Pyramids, Fiction Vixen, Globug & Hootie Need a Book, Hot Coffee Books and Chocobar, Lisa's Book Review, Lisa's Reads, Love Affair With An E-Reader, Madison says, Mama Laughlin, Maryse's Book Blog, Momma's Books, Natasha is a Book Junkie, Romance Book Reviews Blog, Romantic Book Affairs, Romantic Reading Escapes, Scandalicious Book Reviews, Selena-Lost-in-Thought, She Can't Shut Up, Sim-Sational-Books, Talk Supe, Tara's Reads, Teahoney's Book Café, The Autumn Review, The Book List Reviews, The Indie Bookshelf, The Romance Reviews, Totally Booked, Tough Critic Book Reviews, Under the Covers, Unraveling Aira, Up all Night Reviews, What to Read After Fifty (50) Shades of Grey Facebook page.

FUTURES AND FROSTING

TARA SIVEC

1. GREEN JELL-O AND SNAPPING TURTLES

I have a dream.

And in this dream I'm under the covers in bed, just a few scant inches away from Carter's body. I stare at his prone form lying next to me, the greenish-blue glow from the alarm clock on the bedside table providing just enough illumination for me to see the shallow rise and fall of his chest. The sheet is draped low over his hips as he sleeps peacefully with one arm flung over his eyes and the other resting on his taut, naked stomach. I slide my body ever so slowly across the bed, careful not to disturb him, until I'm so close I can feel the heat from his skin warming me from head to toe. I pull my arms out from under the sheet and my hands reach out towards him. I connect with his smooth, muscular chest, slide my fingers up his body, and...choke the ever living shit out of him.

Okay, that's not really a dream. It's more of a wish if you will, something I fantasize about when business is slow at the shop, when I'm waiting in line at the grocery store, or pretty much every waking moment of every single day when I find myself yawning and cranky from lack of sleep. But it's not like I would ever follow through with this fantasy. I love Carter. I really do. Sometimes it's just a toss-up on whether or not I love sleep more.

A few months ago, I hadn't even known Carter existed. Okay, I knew he existed; somewhere out there, over the rainbow, in a land far, far away living his own life. I never believed in a million years that he would ever stop and give me, his one-night-stand from college, a second thought. Turns out I was wrong on both counts. A land far, far away had turned out to be a few miles from where I lived and that second thought I figured he had never given? Well, much to my dismay, and using a Harlequin Romance novel cliché, he had spent years pining for me and searching the world for *'the one that got away'*.

That's me by the way, in case you haven't been paying attention.

Here I am, a twenty-four-year-old single mother to Gavin (the wonderful parting gift I received in appreciation of my mad virginity-giving-up skillz, 'yo) when suddenly, the guy I spontaneously gave said virginity to after a rousing game of beer pong at a frat party shows up in my home town to whisk me off my feet and claim the son he never knew he had. This doesn't happen in real life. Something this perfect only happens in books or John Hughes movies.

Alright, so Carter has never stood outside my window holding a radio above his head and he's never run down the street to sweep me up into his arms for a toe-curling kiss and hand me a pair of diamond earrings he gave to some other skank just moments before. Our story isn't necessarily a textbook eighties movie. There have been anxiety attacks, freak-outs, drunken ramblings, inappropriate cursing, misunderstandings, arguments, two-finger eye-threats, and chocolate covered sex in a public place that only by the hair of a gnat's testicle avoided being publicly televised. Through it all though, Carter and I have managed to work through our problems with the speed an accuracy of a thirty-minute sitcom on prime time television. It's no *"Some Kind of Wonderful,"* but it's damn near close. I'm still waiting for my street kiss and diamond earrings, though.

In the middle of all this chaos, I am also busy following my dream of opening my own candy and cookie shop. I know right? Why not add one more thing to worry about to my growing pile. There's a reason why I have a magnet on my fridge that says, "You can sleep when you're dead."

My best friend Liz and I had always talked of one day owning businesses together. While I was busy with the whole single mom gig and put my aspirations on a back burner, Liz was finishing up college and got a head start on her dream. Little did I know, she had also made plans to assure that my hopes didn't die along with my ability to sneeze and not piss myself.

I've always been a pretty independent person, so having someone hand me my dream in a neat little package with a bow on top took some getting used to. Liz had inherited a good chunk of change from her grandfather when he passed away years earlier and putting that money to good use by purchasing a building where we could have adjoining businesses was the only option for her. It had taken me a few days to get my head out of my ass and realize that she didn't do it out of pity. She had done it because she loves me and having her dream come true wouldn't have meant nearly as much to her if mine wasn't becoming a reality right along with her.

So in summary, I am EXHAUSTED. And I guess that brings us back to my choking fantasy. Living with another human being takes a little getting used to. So far there are only minimal amounts of irritating qualities we find in each other, and we've overcome those obstacles and are still growing strong. I love Carter more than I ever thought possible, and he has proven to be the best father a woman could ever want for her son. But I swear to God, Jesus, Mary, Joseph, and Christ's childhood friend, Biff, that if he doesn't stop waking me up at four-fifty-eight in the morning, every fucking morning, with his buzz saw snoring, I am going to go David Carradine on his ass.

Oh yes, young grasshopper, you shall choke in your sleep.

Although the more I think about it, David Carradine choked *himself* in some weird sex thing, didn't he? I don't think I can convince Carter to choke himself out no matter how naked I get.

I've tried everything to make my nights of sleep less irritating. I've gently pushed his arm so he would roll over because according to Google, a simple change of position will put a halt to the snoring.

False. And shut up, everything on Google is true! How else would I know that the world's oldest living goldfish is forty-one and his name is Fred? Or that when you type the word "askew" in Google search the page will tilt slightly clockwise? These are facts, people!

My dad had told me to try buying a box of nasal strips for Carter to fasten across the bridge of his nose every night before bed.

Didn't work. I woke up the next morning with nasal strips stuck in places where nasal strips should *never* be stuck.

It's all fun and games until you need to lock yourself in the bathroom with tweezers, a mirror, and a flashlight.

I've kicked my feet and smacked my hands against the mattress repeatedly in frustration while whisper-screaming about cock-sucking snorers and their lack of respect for people who sleep quietly, and I've jerked the covers off of him, hit him in the face with his own pillow, that I yanked out from under his head, while plugging his nose.

Hey, don't judge me. I'm losing sleep here.

And I had only plugged his nose long enough for him to start choking on his own spit. As soon as he could speak, he told me all about the dream he was having where he thought he was suffocating and how he realized while he was dream-dying that he forgot to tell me he loved me before he went to sleep. Yes, I felt guilty. Yes, I made it up to him by having sex with him at five in the morning, and no I have never told him that it was me who actually tried to off him in his sleep.

Sometimes couples need a few secrets.

Carter thinks my irritation with his snoring is cute. Of course he does. He's not the one with his ears bleeding in the middle of the night, praying for his bed mate to asphyxiate in his sleep. Oh no, he is off in dreamland, wondering why the soundtrack of his really good sex dream suddenly includes the melody of knives being sharpened.

Last night, one of my well placed kicks to his thigh, er, I mean gentle taps, finally got him to shut up and roll over. It was a thing of beauty. The silent, peaceful tranquility that flowed through the bedroom almost made me weep with joy. Sadly, as soon as I fell asleep and began happily frolicking through my own dreamland, Carter was shaking me awake and asking if

I said something. Because according to him, he had been sleeping like a rock but could have sworn he heard me ask him if the green Jell-O should go in the trunk with the snapping turtles.

A public service announcement for men: If you see that your significant other is fast asleep and your initial whispered question doesn't get a response, don't be surprised if we start spewing green vomit out of the mouths of our rapidly spinning heads as you shake us awake to ask your stupid question fifty decibels louder than the first time.

So here I am again, wide awake at five in the morning, giving the love of my life the stink eye in the dark and wondering if I will be able to keep a straight face when looking at him if I go ahead and order that chin strap contraption I saw on the Home Shopping Network the previous week. As I stare at the ceiling and wonder why a snoring prevention mechanism has to look so much like a jock strap for the face, I suddenly remember something *else* I read on Google not that long ago that I haven't tried yet (Fred, the forty-one-year-old goldfish – FRED IS REAL, dammit!). The article had stated that a short, loud yell of a random, one-syllable word will break through the snoring person's conscience just enough to get them to stop snoring without fully waking them up.

I roll my head to the side to stare at Carter's profile. Watching him sleep soundly while I currently reside in insomnia-land, as a direct result of his deviated septum, makes me feel stabby. Since I can't take my anger out on his septum without making him bleed, I figure I might as well try one more thing. Especially since buying the chin/jock/anti-snoring strap will require that I address Carter as Dick Face from now on. Something I'm assuming he will frown upon.

I take a deep breath and let out my one-syllable word. "F-U-U-U-U-U-C-K!"

In the blink of an eye Carter jolts awake with a scream, flailing his arms and legs and scrambling across the bed until he falls off the side and lands on the floor with a loud thud.

"Son of a bitch! What the hell was that?" he mutters from the floor.

"I think there's green Jell-O in the trunk with the turtles," I state before rolling over and snuggling under the covers.

2. MY DOG HAS THE HUNGRY

"I just don't think it's a good idea, Claire."

I roll my eyes at my dad as I shove a tray of fresh Butter Brickle Bars into the display case under the front counter a little harder than necessary. A few of the bars jump out of their spots on the tray due to my irritation, and as I reach in to fix them, I have to force myself not to eat another one. As much as I love making sweets, I normally don't eat very many. My tastes tend to lean more towards salty snacks. I don't know what is wrong with me lately though. If I keep sampling the goods like this my ass is going to grow another cheek to make room for all the fat.

"I really don't think you've thought this through," my dad continues as he leans his hip against the counter and folds his arms across his chest.

I take that back. I know exactly why I've been pigging out on chocolate and cookies.

I reached into the glass case and grab the Butter Brickle Bar closest to me and shovel the whole thing in my mouth at once. I take a moment to savor the taste of brown sugar, vanilla, and toffee bits, letting the sugary sweetness do its trick of removing some of my stress. Since I can't physically chuck the six-foot-two tension problem I currently have out of the store without giving myself a hernia, this will have to do. I swallow the mouthful of cookie bar and try not to think about it forming little legs and sprinting straight to my ass, leaving pats of butter behind on my hips as it goes. I take a deep, fortifying breath so I can deal with my father.

"Dad, Carter and I have been living together for two months. It's a little late for this speech now don't you think?"

My dad has never said one word for or against mine and Carter's living arrangements ever since we first announced it on the day of Seduction and Snacks' grand opening.

He had grunted, glared at Carter, and then walked away. That was approval as far as I had been concerned.

Now that it's been two months and I haven't changed my mind like he probably thought I would, suddenly he has an opinion.

"Everyone says, 'why buy the bar when you can get the beer for free'."

I stop with my arm in midair as I reach for a towel to wipe down the counter.

"Dad, no one says that."

"*Everyone* says that," he replies, pushing himself away from the counter and moving his hands to his hips.

I roll my eyes and began wiping crumbs off of the top of the display case.

"Really? Who?" I challenge as the bell above the door chimes and a customer walks in.

"People," he states firmly.

I sighed and turn away from my dad to smile and greet the woman who is perusing the white chocolate section at the opposite end of the case from where we are standing. After making sure she doesn't have any questions, I glance back at him.

"Dad, it's two-thousand-and-twelve, not the nineteen-fifties. People live together all the time before they make any kind of huge commitment. We just need some time to get used to each other and learn to live together as a family without killing each other. It's not that big of a deal."

My dad huffs and it is his turn to stare at me in irritation.

"Really, Claire, when have I ever given you any kind of indication that I'm old fashioned? I just don't want this yahoo to think he can move you and Gavin into his place and then never have to do anything to make it official. At least if he married you, I wouldn't have to worry about your whiny ass showing up on my doorstep anytime soon wanting your old room back."

I wonder how many Butter Brickle Bars I can fit in my mouth at one time.

18

"Did you really just call Carter a *yahoo*? How about we take a seat on the davenport so we can discuss that little hooligan and how you aren't old fashioned in the least?" I state sarcastically.

"I should have sold you to that traveling circus when you were four. I could be out on the lake fishing right now instead of having this conversation," he mutters.

My dad had been married twice before he married my mom, and he had his first wife Linda's name tattooed on his arm. When I was younger I tried to change Linda to my mom's name, Rachel, with a sharpie marker when he was sleeping. Unfortunately, he woke up before I could finish. It took him three days to wash Rinda off of his arm. When I told that story to Carter, he started singing like the Chinese men in *"A Christmas Story"*. *Deck da hars with boughs of horry, fa-ra-ra-ra-ra, ra-ra-ra-ra*! He tried joking with my dad once about it saying, "You reary roved Rinda." My dad thought he was impersonating Scooby Doo and didn't find it funny. Could be why he wasn't one hundred percent sold on the whole living together situation. And all of it was a prime example of why I wasn't jumping on board the marriage band wagon just yet. My dad had struck out three times and my mom twice when she had finally decided marriage wasn't for her when I was twelve and packed up to get a condo in the city.

I don't really have shining examples of happily ever after in my life.

Anyway, the point is everyone makes their own decisions about life, some good and some bad. They all teach us something about who we are and blah, blah, blah. No matter what my dad's opinion is, I need to know if Carter's snoring and his inability to put a new roll of toilet paper back on the holder is going to be a deal breaker before we do something legal that we can't back out of.

So far, stupid bad habits aside, we are doing quite well cohabiting. Gavin has adjusted nicely, and I haven't smothered Cater in his sleep. That's total win right there.

My dad can finally tell by the look on my face that I am closing the conversation for further discussion or arguments, and he has given up on the beer/sex/whatever the fuck analogy. He grabs the newspaper he set down on the counter when he first walked in, tucks it under his arm, and walks over to one of the small tables by the front window to drink his coffee. Regardless of the mood he had put me in, seeing the four black, round tables set up in front of the picture window at the front of the store makes me smile. They had just been delivered the prior week and seeing someone sitting in them, even if it is my father, made me giddy. This is *my* store and those are *my* tables and nothing can mar the elated feeling that gave me.

The chime above the door sounds again, and I glanced over to see my friend Jenny storm in with an angry scowl on her face. Never in a million years have I ever picture myself being friends with someone like her. She is runway model beautiful and the things that come out of her mouth rarely make sense, but she's proven to be a good friend in the few months since I've met her and would help anyone with anything they asked without a second thought. Much to everyone's surprise, Jenny had managed to grab onto Carter's best friend, Drew, and wrap him around her little finger. Drew is the biggest man whore you will ever lay eyes on, but for whatever reason, Jenny is able to tame him. Somewhat.

"Hey, what's going on?" I ask Jenny as I round the counter to meet her halfway. I glance down at my watch and see it's only eleven in the morning. "Why aren't you at work?"

Jenny works for the same computer design company she has since her freshman year in college.

She had started off as an intern and quickly made her way up the ranks and was now one of the most talented graphic designers they had on staff. She helped me out in a pinch when I was opening my store and made all of the flyers, brochures, and business cards in her free time and refused to take any payment. It had been one of the main reasons I decided I liked her.

Anyone who doesn't charge me for services rendered is good people in my book.

Jenny laughs manically at my question about work and crossed her arms in front of her. "That's a great question, Claire. And the answer would be, I got fired," she replies before bursting into tears, flinging her arms around me, and burying her face in my shoulder.

Oh Jesus God no.

I awkwardly bend my elbow and pat my hand against her lower back. She still has her arms wrapped around me in a vice grip and that's as high as I can reach. I shove my other hand into the pocket of my jeans and pull out my cell phone, sending a quick "please help me, God" text to Liz next door.

Jenny continues to cry, sniffle and every few minutes wail. After subtly spitting out some of her hair from my mouth as she burrows further into my neck and shoulder, I anxiously glance down at my cell phone wondering how much longer I will need to pretend I enjoy soothing people during breakdowns before Liz gets her ass over here and rescues me. It probably won't be very friend-like of me if I start freaking out that there might now be a pile of someone else's snot pooling on the shoulder of my tee-shirt. My phone buzzes in my hand and I crane my neck over Jenny's shoulder to see the message.

I am busy with customers. You are going to have to MAN UP and comfort her yourself. Start acting like you have a vagina for fuck's sake and hug her.
XOXO – Liz

I grit my teeth at the knowledge I am on my own in the pits of consoling hell.

"There, there," I say, patting her on the back again. I really think I should have been born a guy. I don't know many women who get skeeved out by displays of emotion. If I see a woman crying, I usually run in the other direction. I am not one of those people that throws my arms around her and tells her everything will be okay—because it probably won't. It will most likely suck just as much whether I hug you or not, so it's probably best for everyone involved if I just stand off to the side and let someone else do the touching. I feel much more comfortable wallowing in anger and stewing about something privately until my head explodes. That's natural. Hugging and crying and snotting all over someone isn't.

"Didn't you just get a raise? Why in the hell would they fire you?" I ask as I worm my way out of her arms and try to subtly back away from her.

Don't look at the snot on your shoulder, don't look at the snot on your shoulder. I know you can feel it there, but for God's sakes, DON'T LOOK AT IT!

Jenny finally releases her hold on me and uses the back of her hands to wipe the tear streaks off her face. If only she would have done that with the snot instead of using my shoulder.

"I don't have any idea why they really fired me. They gave me some song and dinner about positive attitude." she pouts.

"You mean dance?" I ask in confusion.

"Claire, focus! I got fired! This is no time for talk about dancing," she yells.

I take a deep, calming breath and put my hands on my hips to keep from strangling her.

"Okay, so they fired you because they didn't like your attitude?" I reiterate.

Jenny looks at me incredulously. "I know, right? I told them I was the most positive person in that dump."

"Verbatim?" I ask her.

"I didn't forbid them anything. What are you talking about? Are you even listening? Have you been drinking?"

The last is stated in a stage whisper as she looks over at the customer who came in earlier. I pinch the bridge of my nose and try not to stomp my foot and throw a temper tantrum like Gavin does when I tell him he is grounded from PlayStation.

"What am I going to do without a job?" she whines as she paces back and forth in front of me. "It's mine and Drew's three month anniversary and I was going to buy him something really special and now I'm not going to be able to afford it."

I grab onto her elbow to stop her pacing and pulled her back behind the counter with me when I saw the customer was finally ready to order.

"I'm sure Drew will understand," I tell her as I start filling a box with the woman's request of a pound of white chocolate covered pretzels.

"No he won't. He's going to be so upset. I already told him what I was buying, and he was really looking forward to the vagina mold," she says dejectedly.

I drop the metal candy scoop on the floor and look over at Jenny as she sighs miserably.

As I pick up the scoop and toss it into the sink before grabbing a clean one, all sorts of thoughts swirl through my mind that shouldn't be when I am waiting on a customer—like who-ha's covered in green fuzz and moldy cheese vaginas dancing around the Tupperware container in the back of my fridge with two-month old spaghetti in it.

Jenny looks over and sees the horror on my face as I try to block out the mental image of moldy cheese vaginas singing, "Mold, mold, baby," in the voice of Vanilla Ice in my head.

"Claire, didn't you see the new product Liz got in last week? It's a mold you can make of your vagina. So your guy can...you know..."

Jenny uses the age old finger gesture of a penis going into a vagina by making a circle with her index finger and thumb and using the index finger of her other hand to move in and out of it.

"Eeeew, what? That's disgusting," I whisper, smacking her hands to get her to stop making that motion with her fingers as I hand the customer her chocolate.

"It's not disgusting," Jenny says. "It's romantic. Drew wants a replica of my..." she glances at the customer and then lowers her voice "...love tunnel so he can be with me whenever we're apart."

I step away from her to ring up the customer, trying not to picture Drew holding on to some little floppy, silicone vagina-looking thing, talking to it in a baby voice like it's Jenny. *"Oooooh, I wuv my wittle fake Jenny-vagina! Yes I do!"*

"Wouldn't it be easier to just get him a blow-up doll and tape your picture over its face?" I ask as I watch the customer leave the store with her purchase and hope she didn't hear enough of this conversation to prevent her from ever stepping foot in here again.

Jenny shakes her head at me in pity. "You have absolutely no sense of romance, Claire."

I huff in indignation as I get busy filling a box with chocolate covered strawberries for an order that's being picked up after lunch. I am plenty romantic.

Just this morning while he slept, I had left Carter a box of his favorite candy next to his pillow–Globs: piles of white chocolate covered, crushed potato chips and pretzels drizzled with caramel. I figured it would soften him up to the note I placed next to the box telling him if he left the toilet seat up one more time and my ass got an involuntary bath at six in the morning, I would put super glue on the head of his penis while he slept. I had even signed the note with a couple of Xs and Os.

Who says romance is dead?

I close up the box of strawberries and finish it off with my signature pink bow and a sticker with the name and address of the store. Setting it aside, I turn to face Jenny and find her inhaling an entire pan of white chocolate covered Nutter Butter cookies that I had been experimenting with that morning.

"Jenny, put the chocolate down and step away from the tray slowly." I speak to her in my best hostage negotiator voice. "I wanted to ask you if you'd be able to help out with a few things for me, but I knew you were busy with work," I explain as I reach around her and take the tray from her hands before she harms herself or others with her unemployment gluttony.

"Work!" Jenny says with a whimper as her lip starts to quiver. She reaches out with both hands and grabs back onto the tray of half-empty chocolates.

"Oh Jesus, will you let me finish?!" I scold as I smack her hands.

She sighs and finally lets go of the tray of chocolates, spitting out a half-eaten Nutter Butter into the middle of the pile before she turns to face me.

"Those are delicious, but I feel kind of pukey right now," she mumbles, putting a hand to her stomach.

I move the tray far out of her reach and my line of sight before I myself become pukey.

"As I was saying, I have a bunch of things you could do for me here. I need a website created and maintained, advertising managed, and everything that goes along with marketing this place that I know nothing about. I got a call just the other day from a magazine wanting to set up an interview, and I have no idea what I'm doing. I know it's not your ideal job, and I probably can't pay you anywhere near as much as you're used to making, but in the interim, until you find something else, would you like to work for me?"

The squeal that erupts from Jenny breaks the sound barrier and makes small dogs throughout the land howl in terror. She throws her arms around me and bounces up and down, making me feel uncomfortable once again at the displays of affection people feel the need to give.

"Thank you so much, Claire! I promise you won't be disappointed. I will do such a good job you'll want to bang the shit out of me!"

I glance up to see my dad standing behind Jenny looking like he'd rather eat the regurgitated chocolate covered Nutter Butter at that moment than inadvertently hear our conversation.

"I just…I'm gonna…my dog has the hungry," he mumbles before turning and walking away.

Jenny lets go of me and watches as he quickly exits the shop. "You're dad has a dog?"

I shook my head and let out a deep sigh. "Nope."

3. HE WENT TO JARED

"Hey, Carter, when I drunk dialed you last night, did I by any chance mention where I put my keys?" Drew asks as I walk into the living room.

He rummages through the couch cushions, cursing and pulling out loose change, McDonald Happy Meal toys, and other goodies he finds in the cracks and crevices. I grab my baseball cap off of one of the end tables and stick it on my head before turning to watch him.

Drew and I haven't shared a living space in months, yet somehow, even now that Claire and I are living together, I still manage to find him passed out on my couch every once in a while.

"How did you even get home last night if you didn't have your keys? And I hope you know that I use the term "home" loosely. As much as I enjoy your company and watching you stumble drunkenly around my home at four in the morning when Jenny won't answer her door because she thinks you're an axe murderer, this is not where you live. Even though you might think so since I always seem to answer the door and let you in."

A cell phone sails out of the couch as Drew continues to dig to China in search of his keys. I walk over and scoop it up, putting it in my back pocket. Now I remember why I let Drew in the door. He isn't afraid to stick his hand down into the bottom of a couch. I had known exactly where I lost my cell phone; I was just too afraid to go in search of it. There are scary, scary things living in the bottom of those cushions. Something I had quickly found out was a direct result of living with a child.

"I probably took a cab. Or walked. I don't know, the evening got a little fuzzy after I found produce stickers on my penis when I went to take a piss," he replies in all seriousness as he gets up from his knees and turns to face me. The wrinkled and stained shirt he wears that states, "Ask me about my huge

27

penis," has one of the sleeves torn off and proves he had a rough night.

I don't even bother trying to tell him that if he didn't have his keys when he left the club or wherever he ended up last night, it stands to reason they won't be hibernating in my couch. I have other things on my mind at the moment though. I walk away from Drew and into the kitchen, making my way to my coat that's hanging on the back of one of the chairs. I reach into the inside pocket, pull out the small, black velvet box, and open the lid to look inside for the ten thousandth time since I picked it up last week.

The sight of the one and a half carat, platinum, diamond ring nestled in the white satin makes my heart pound with excitement. And I'm not going to lie; it also makes me want to throw up in my mouth. Just a little bit. I stare down at the precious metal that that took me eight days and six trips to the jewelry store to pick out. The main diamond is princess cut and framed by twelve, three-quarter carat round diamonds. The ring is complimented by lines of round diamonds along the band. It's elegant and beautiful.

Yes, I know I sound like a walking advertisement for a jewelry store and men everywhere are humming the tune of "Taps" right now and brain screaming, "MAN DOWN!" but I feel a little fist pump is in order due to the fact that Claire will be able to look over at her friends all smug-like and say, "He went to Jared!"

If she says yes. Which she totally will, ha ha! I'm not nervous at all. I don't feel all itchy and ball-sweaty thinking about popping the question and the possibility that she just might laugh in my face and tell me I'm bat shit crazy. Who gets married after only being together a few months? Who has a one-night-stand in college and finds out five years later it resulted in a child? Who spends all those years turning into a creeper that stalks bath and body shops every time they get a new chocolate-scented lotion line and gets a hard-on at work when some guy, whose wife just had a baby girl, passed out Hershey bars with the cutesy little wrapper that says, "HERESHEIS!"

This guy right here. Don't even ask how I explained away the boner and how I am NOT a child molester and that it's totally natural to get turned on when a co-worker is talking about a baby.

That sentence sounded much better in my head, so let's just pretend I never said it and move on.

The fact is, I spent years wishing I could see my one-night-stand again and find out if she was real, hoping I could one day meet her again and see if she could still make me laugh and turn me on with just a brush of her hand or the smell of her skin.

I had tried to fill the void with a woman whose mouth could hold more balls than a Hungry, Hungry Hippo, but walking in on her playing hide the salami with our neighbor made me realize two things. One, I should have never tried to blot out the memory of my dream girl with someone else. And by "someone else" I meant a whore. And two, our neighbor had Elephantitis of the ball and should seriously get that looked at by a medical professional of some sort. And no, that wasn't a mistake. I really meant *ball*, as in singular. Dude only had one ball and it was the size of a coconut.

Seriously. Google a picture of a coconut. I'll wait. Because you really need to get the full effect of what I saw dangling there for the twenty seconds it took for me to get my head out of my ass and scream insults at both of them.

All of this, while nightmare inducing, had made me realize that when I found Claire, I knew I would do whatever it took to never lose her again.

We may have done everything ass backwards, but I wouldn't change a thing. Claire and Gavin are my whole world and I want to make it official. I want her to know that nothing could tear me away from them and that I am in it for the long haul. Pushing the nerves aside, I smile as I stare at my future and a big chunk of my savings account tucked into the small, velvet box. I close the lid with a *snap* just as Drew walks into the kitchen dangling his keys from the tip of his index finger, holding them out away from his body as far as possible.

"So you're really going to do it, huh? You're going to make an honest woman out of Claire?" he asks as he runs water in the sink, dumps in about a half a bottle of liquid soap, and throws his keys into the growing pile of bubbles. He shuts the water off and turns around to lean against the counter. I give him and the sink a questioning look and he just shrugs his shoulders.

"I found them in the tank of the toilet. Better to be safe than sorry."

Gavin chooses that moment to run into the room and I lift him up into my arms before I can ask Drew why this is the second time in a month he's lost his keys in my toilet.

"Why is Uncle Drew washing dishes?" Gavin asks as he wrapped his arms around my neck.

"I'm not washing dishes. I'm washing my keys," Drew explains with his back to us as he splashes in the water trying to retrieve them. He flings them out of the sink as he turns back around, splattering Gavin and I with suds.

"You don't wash keys. That's dumb," Gavin replies seriously.

"Um, hello? You do too wash keys. Especially if they have *your* poop on them because they were in *your* toilet," Drew replies as he shakes the excess suds off of his key ring.

"I don't poop on keys! YOU poop on keys!" Gavin yells angrily. "I'm going to stick your head in the toilet!"

I probably should have intervened by now, but sometimes this is the highlight of my day. I unwind Gavin's arms from my neck and set him back down.

"Okay, that's enough. Gavin, go in your room and get your baseball hat. It's almost time to pick up mommy and go to the game."

Gavin takes off running but not before giving Drew a dirty look.

"Dude, that kid has anger issues. I hope you sleep with one eye open at night," Drew mutters as he watches Gavin run off. He turns back to face me and crosses his arms in front of him. "So, you took my suggestion and went with the baseball game proposal. Nice. Good work."

"As much as it pains me to say this, it was a really good idea. A guy at work got a bunch of free tickets to the Indian's game today because his daughter works for the concierge desk at Progressive Field. According to this guy, they don't allow you to just pay for a proposal to be put up on the scoreboard anymore. He gave me his daughter's work number and she told me about this whole proposal package they have. So, for three hundred dollars I am now the proud owner of a Cleveland Indian's Proposal Package," I explain proudly.

"Will those three hundred dollars assure that they might actually win a game this year?" Drew asks.

I shake my head. "Probably not. But, it does get us moved to VIP seating in a loge after I propose, a five-by-seven glossy photo of the proposal as it was seen on the scoreboard, a dozen red roses, and a gift certificate to the Terrace Club restaurant right at the park so we can have dinner to celebrate," I say with a smile as I grab my non-toilet-infested car keys off of the counter along with my wallet.

"If she says yes, you mean. Otherwise that's just going to be the most depressing photo you will ever have hanging on your wall and a *really* uncomfortable dinner," Drew supplies with a sad shake of his head.

"Thank you so much for that vote of confidence," I deadpan.

And now the nerves are back. But I won't let them get to me. I've been wracking my brain for weeks trying to come up with a unique and special way to propose to Claire, and when she mentioned casually that she'd never taken Gavin to an Indian's game, I knew it would be the perfect setting. It will be in front of thousands of people and our son will be there to witness it. What could be better than that? And really, what woman wouldn't love it?

~

During the sixth inning is when everything went to shit. Aside from the Drew-induced nervous stomach I suffered from during the first five innings, we are having a great time. Gavin is amazed by the ballpark and the Indians were up by seven. As my knee bounces up and down, and I force myself not to buy another hot dog to give myself something to do because eight ballpark hot dogs is where I draw the line, I try not to think about the fact that I never asked Claire's father for her hand in marriage. That is something people still did nowadays, isn't it? Would George be mad at me that I didn't have a formal sit-down with him to discuss our upcoming nuptials and whether or not he approved? And now that I have said the word, "sit-down," I am having flashes of George wearing a three-piece suit and fedora staring at me across a plate of half-eaten linguini while he steeples his fingers under his chin and then excuses himself to go to the bathroom so he can get the gun he hid behind the toilet and shoot me in the head.

"Leave the gun. Take the cannoli!"

A few people in the row in front of us turn around to look at me quizzically and I just shrug. They won't judge me if they know my future father-in-law is a mobster who wants me dead for not going through the proper channels to marry his one and only daughter.

Claire is too busy arguing with Gavin about how a third bag of cotton candy will not, in fact, give him superpowers no matter what he saw on television so she has no idea about the minor freak-out I had going on. Not that I would talk to her about it anyway. This is supposed to be a surprise—a huge, life-changing surprise that could make or break our future. Or my kneecaps if George decides he really does hate me.

I continue my manic foot tapping as Jose Cabrera goes up to the plate and repeat the words I plan to say to Claire in my head.

32

I never thought I'd find you again...you are my heart and soul and my reason for living...every moment I spend with you is like-

Claire's laughter breaks my concentration, and I glance over to see her pointing to the outfield and snickering with a few people sitting around her.

"Oh my God, would you look at that!" she exclaims.

I glance out beyond third base to see what has caught her interest. When I see what everyone else is staring at, my stomach plummets all the way to my toes and the eight hotdogs I just consumed threaten to make a reappearance in a totally unflattering way that won't be near as much fun as dancing meat singing the Oscar Mayer wiener song.

There, televised on the jumbotron for all of Progressive Field to see, is a guy down on one knee somewhere by the first base line holding up a ring box to a hysterically sobbing woman with her hands over her mouth in shock. In big, jumbotron-sized, blinking red letters below their picture are the words, "Crystal, will you marry me? Love Rob!"

Claire snorts and shakes her head. "What a tool that guy is. How cheesy can you be? Proposing at a baseball game in front of tens of thousands of strangers and putting it up on the scoreboard? That's got to be the most clichéd thing ever.

"REALLY ORIGINAL THERE, MORON!" she yells as everyone around us claps and cheers when the woman on the screen nods her head up and down emphatically and the pair embrace.

Oh sweet Jesus. Sweet mother fucking fuckery of fucks.

I am going to win the *'Tool of the Year'* award if my proposal shows up on that screen in the next five minutes like it's scheduled to. I don't even know if there *is* a *'Tool of the Year'* award. There must be. It's probably a huge, gold penis trophy with an arrow pointing to it that reads, "This is you! A giant dick! Congratulations." There's probably even a *'Tool of the Year'* book they print every year like that *'Darwin*

33

Awards' book that really has nothing to do with winning an esteemed award and everything to do with the fact that people are pointing and laughing because you died from trying to slow dance with an ostrich that would rather peck out your eyes than learn the Cha Cha.

Claire is going to peck out my eyes if I propose to her right now!

"Carter, are you okay? You look like you're going to throw up. I told you no one should ever eat more than six hotdogs. That's just asking for pig snout disease or whatever the hell they make those things out of," Claire scolds as she looked me over worriedly.

"I ate a pig snout?!" Gavin asks elatedly. "What's a pig snout?

Claire turns to the other side of her to try and explain to Gavin that hotdogs are, in fact, not made out of dogs, and I take that moment to jump up from my seat, mumbling something about throwing up before I race up the stairs to the concierge desk to cancel my Cleveland Indian's Proposal Package before I die a slow, horrible eye-pecking death.

4. HE LOVES ME, HE LOVES ME NOT

"I think he's going to break up with me."

Liz's sigh through the phone line is loud and clear. I know she's irritated with me. *I* am irritated with me. It's getting to the point where I can't even stand the sound of my own voice and yet I can't shut up about this.

"He's been acting really weird ever since the Indian's game last week," I explain as I pull my car into the driveway and let the engine idle.

"Carter isn't going to break up with you. Will you shut up about this already? Maybe he's just stressed about work or the fact that his parents are finally coming for a visit. Did you try out that move on him I told you about the other night? The one where you take your fingers and put them in his-"

"LA-LA-LA, I'M NOT LISTENING TO YOU!" I yell over her voice and try to block out the words "prostate" and "gentle massage".

"Fine, but I'm telling you – it will totally relax him," she says matter-of-factly.

I turn off the ignition and rested my head against the steering wheel.

"Have you tried, oh I don't know, *asking* him what's wrong?" Liz continues.

"You're rolling your eyes at me right now, aren't you?" I reply. "No, I haven't asked him. I've done what every other woman in a new relationship does when her boyfriend is acting all twitchy and nervous. I completely ignore the situation and pretend like it isn't happening while making a list of possible responses and comebacks I can lob at him when he finally decides to give me the brush-off. I am NOT going to be one of those people who clam up when he tells me, 'It's not you, it's me,' and then six hours later when I'm sitting alone in the dark with a bottle of vodka scream, 'OH IT'S TOTALLY YOU AND YOUR SMALL PENIS!'. I'm going to have viable retorts ready to go so I don't come up with them later when I'm drunk and alone, and they do no one any good."

I sit back in my seat and stare at the front door of the house I now live in with Carter. The white, three bedroom ranch with black shutters is nestled in a lush cluster of pine trees. I love this house. But more importantly, I love the two men inside of it. My heart literally hurts to think about not being with Carter.

"Carter doesn't have a small penis, by the way," I say, breaking the silence.

"So you've told me. Several times," Liz deadpans.

"I'm sorry I keep bugging you about this."

"Don't apologize. That's what I'm here for. Just talk to him about it. You can thank me for my sage advice by remembering that, as my maid of honor, you are required to keep any and all passé bachelorette party activities as far away from me as possible this weekend," Liz reminds me.

Liz and Jim's wedding date is fast approaching. Being as far removed from a typical bride as possible, Liz had vetoed a traditional bachelorette party and instead decided it would just be one big co-ed night out. Maybe that's what Carter and I need - a night out with friends without any work or parenting responsibilities. I thank Liz again and quickly hang up the phone so I can go in the house and greet my boys.

~

"I'm home!" I yell as I close the front door behind me and set my purse down on the table next to it.

A flash of color darts into the room and barrels into me.

"Mommy's home!" Gavin cheers as I pick him up and start walking further into the house.

"Where's Daddy?" I ask as I rub his back while he clings to me.

"He's gettin' ready for work."

36

I walk into the bedroom and set him down on top of the bed, bouncing onto the mattress next to him. Gavin stands up and starts jumping up and down and singing.

"Woke up dis mornin', got myself a gun!"

Before I can tell him to stop, Carter walks out of the bathroom, popping his head through the neck of a tee shirt and then pulling the material the rest of the way down over his stomach.

"Hey, baby," he greets me with a smile as he makes his way over to the bed, leans over, and gives me a kiss. He lingers against my mouth and rubs his lips back and forth against mine before pulling away so he can look at me.

"Did you let our son watch *The Sopranos'* again today? I ask him with a raise of my eyebrows.

Carter laughs nervously and backs away. "No, why would you think that?"

Gavin stops bouncing on the bed and looks at Carter.

"Yes you did, Daddy. Don't you wemember? Big Pussy cried and you called him a pansy-ass," he says earnestly.

I look at Carter pointedly.

"And tell me you didn't take him out in public today with that shirt on."

We both look at Gavin's shirt that boldly states, "They shake me."

"I can neither confirm nor deny those rumors," Carter says as he sits down next to me on the bed so he can put his shoes on. "Let's just say we had lunch with Uncle Drew, and if I didn't put the new shirt on Gavin that he bought him, there would have been a scene."

"I'm pretty sure Gavin would have been fine if you refrained from putting him in that shirt," I tell him.

"I'm not talking about Gavin. Have you *met* Drew?"

Gavin takes a leap off of the bed and runs out of the room. I scoot closer to Carter and rest my head on his shoulder. He lifts one arm and wraps it around my shoulder, pulling me against his side. He seems okay

37

right now, so I figure there is no need to ruin the moment and ask him what his problem has been the past few days and if he still loves me.

"Sometimes I really hate that you work nights," I tell him softly, wrapping my arms around his waist.

He turns and kisses me, easing both of us back onto the bed so we are laying in a tangle of legs and arms.

"You don't have to lie. I know you like the peace and quiet during the week and having control over the remote," he says with a smile as he brushes a piece of hair out of my eyes.

"You're right, I do. But it doesn't mean I don't love you. It just means *'The Real Housewives of Orange County'* can be watched without eye rolls and sarcastic comments. If anyone is going to judge Gretchen and Slade for their poor life choices it will be me," I explain.

"Oh, that reminds me. I've got something for you," he says as he pulled his arms out from around me and rolls onto his back so he can dig into the pocket of his jeans.

"Are you going to tell me that you have a present in your pants for me? Because I've got to tell you, I've been to that pants party a bunch of times. I almost got a concussion last time."

Carter digs deeper into his pocket and huffs at me.

"It is not my fault I was unprepared for road-head. I thought you weren't feeling good and were just going to put your head down in my lap. When a man's penis suddenly makes an appearance in a moving vehicle on a Saturday night, an involuntary hip thrust WILL HAPPEN."

He finally pulls his hand out of his pocket and holds it out to me, palm up.

"This is your present," he says to me.

I look into his hand to see two small, orange, bell-shaped pieces of foam resting inside of a tiny plastic bag. I look at them quizzically trying to decide the correct response one should have when receiving something that looked like dresses for Polly Pocket dolls.

"Um, you shouldn't have?"

Carter laughs at my obvious confusion.

"Oh I should have. Especially if I want to live through another night of sleeping next to you. These, my dear, are the best earplugs ever. They have bins and bins of them at work. If you like them, let me know and I'll bring a bunch more home."

He got me earplugs. He really DOES love me.

I take the bag from his hand and tear open the plastic with my teeth so I can pull the squishy orange plugs out and look them over. I roll one between my finger and thumb to shrink it, and then I push it into my ear.

I repeat the process with the other one and lie perfectly still as the foam slowly expanded until I can't hear a single sound except for the *whoosh* of my breathing.

"THANK YOU SO MUCH, THESE ARE PERFECT!" I tell him.

At least I assume that's what I said. To me it had sounded more like the teacher in a Charlie Brown cartoon.

Carter smiles and I see his mouth move.

"WHAT?"

His mouth moves again.

Does he not understand the concept of earplugs? The word itself is pretty self-explanatory. Ear. Plug. From the Latin root, "I can't hear a fucking thing that is coming out of your mouth."

I stick my finger in my ear and yank one of the plugs out.

"As I was saying, you're welcome. I have to go to work now. Does this ensure that I can go to sleep from now on knowing all of my appendages will still be attached when I wake up?"

He pushes himself up off of the bed, and I pull the other ear plug out and toss them both on my nightstand so I can follow him out of the room.

"I do solemnly swear not to Lorena Bobbet your penis," I tell him as we make our way down the hall and out into the living room.

Carter says a quick good-bye to Gavin who is sitting on the couch watching cartoons and then grabs his work bag off of the floor beside the front door.

"Don't forget Liz and Jim's co-ed pre-wedding party, that we are never to refer to as a bachelor-slash-bachelorette party, is this weekend," I remind Carter as I plant a kiss on his cheek.

"I know. Drew already sent me three texts since lunch trying to get me to admit that I was joking when I told him there wouldn't be strippers. I got a call from his phone after the last text I sent but he never spoke. I think he was just silently weeping in the background."

Carter opens the door and then turns back to me before walking out.

"Oh and don't *you* forget that my parents are coming in this weekend from Columbus. I can't wait for you to finally meet them!"

I close the door behind him and lean my back against it.

"Yay. Meeting the in-laws," I cheer to myself in a completely non-cheery way.

5. SUCK FOR A BUCK

Friday night is finally here and the work week is over. Not that I really have anything to complain about in that regard. I own my own business (someone pinch me!), and every moment I spend in the shop makes me happy. But even when you love what you do, it's still nice to forget about it for a few hours.

The minor freak-outs about Carter are pushed to the back of my mind since everything has been so perfect between us the last couple of days. He doesn't jump when I walk into the room anymore, and he isn't whispering on the phone when I get out of the shower. A normal woman would probably suspect cheating, but not me. I had already followed him a few times and checked his text messages.

Seriously. Don't judge me.

Gavin is spending the night at my dad's house, so as soon as I get home from work, I pack his overnight bag and then got ready for the party. I still haven't stopped thanking Liz after she informed me that she didn't want a traditional bachelorette party where a group of girls get in a limo and go to a strip club.

Thank God.

Don't get me wrong, I'm all for getting liquored up and heading to a female strip club, but a male one? That's just gross. Have you been to an all male strip club before? These oily, long-haired, jacked up on steroid men come prancing out in banana hammocks, thrust their hips in your face, and dry hump your leg. It's disgusting. Have you ever had a sweaty man you don't know rub his penis on your knee? It makes me throw up in my mouth a little just thinking about it. And let's be honest here, the penis – not the prettiest thing in the world to look at. If it's some guy who calls himself the Italian Stallion, wearing a Speedo with the Italian flag on it, dancing to the theme song from *'The Jersey Shore',* while he has one foot up on your knee and hip thrusts his dangling... Okay, I'm just going to stop myself right there before Carter finds me curled up

41

in the fetal position in the corner mumbling about Italian penis, and he thinks I'm saying "penne" and doesn't understand why pasta is making me cry.

As I was saying, Liz doesn't want any of that. She wants to rent a nice limo bus and go to a few local wineries. I'm pretty sure the evening will still include inappropriate behavior, but at least it won't also include ruining a man's self esteem by pointing and laughing at his junk. Unless of course Drew decides to get naked for some reason. I can't be responsible for my actions at that point and it won't be my fault of he cries.

Once Carter and I are dressed and ready to go, we placed Gavin in the car and head over to my dad's to drop him off.

When we stop at a red light, Carter takes one hand off of the wheel and places it on the inside of my bare thigh.

"You wore that short skirt just to torture me, didn't you?" Carter asks softly so Gavin won't hear him from the backseat.

"I have no idea what you're talking about," I say with a smirk as I cross my legs. The movement forced his warm hand higher up my thigh and his fingers graze just under the hem of the tattered jean skirt material.

I'm not lying when I say I kind of enjoy the fact that Carter and I work opposite shifts. I like the peace and quiet during the week and spending alone time with Gavin. It makes the adjustment from being a single mother to living with the father of my child not so bad. I had spent so many years on my own and having my son all to myself, it was nice we weren't thrust right into something that was a complete one-eighty from what we were used to. Even so, it doesn't stop me from missing Carter during the week.

Or more specifically, missing having sex with Carter during the week.

When you have sex once, get pregnant, and then go years before you ever have it again and when you *do* have it again, it's mind-blowing and delicious and better than finding a pot of gold, a unicorn, and a leprechaun who shits diamonds at the end of a rainbow, having to wait a whole week in between having this wonderful sex is torture. Just having Carter's hand on my leg puts all sorts of dirty thoughts in my head - thoughts that have no business being there when our son was in the backseat.

"I think you and I are going to need to make an *important phone call* tonight," Carter says with a wag of his eyebrows.

I laugh, remembering the first time we had sex again after the night he took my virginity at the frat party.

When Gavin had knocked on the bedroom door right at the tail end of our *reunion* (emphasis on union) and then asked us what we were up to, in a panic I told him we were making phone calls. It had seemed like a good idea at the time.

I place my hand on top of Carter's and slide it just a little bit further under the edge of my skirt.

"You missed a lot of *phone calls* this week while you were at work. I had to take care of them on my own. My *phone* has a dead battery now," I tease him.

"Did you record these *phone calls*? That's something I'd like to listen to," he says with a wink before turning his focus back to the road as the light turns green.

"Sorry, the *answering machine* doesn't have a battery either," I joke.

"Probably because you took the batteries out of every single major appliance in a five-mile-radius and put them in your *phone*," Carter replies with a sneer.

"Don't be jealous because the *phone* gets more time with me during the week than you do," I console him with a pat on his hand.

"I'm not jealous. I just used my *Palm PDA*."

I roll my eyes at him.

"Your *Palm PDA* is no match for my...*Vtech Cordless*," I stammer.

What are we even talking about anymore? Is there a point when innuendos jump the shark?

"I know what you guys are doin' when you make a phone call," Gavin pipes up nonchalantly from the backseat.

You know how when you've told a lie and someone catches you in it your face gets all hot and you get butterflies in your stomach? It's ten times worse when it's your own freaking toddler calling you out and looking at you like, "Are you kidding me with this shit?"

"Heh, heh! What do you mean, buddy?" Carter asks, laughing nervously.

He looks at me and I look at him, and we both look in the backseat at Gavin. Thank God we are stopped at another red light. I don't think Carter can be trusted to keep the car in our lane at this moment. Frankly, I don't think *I* can be trusted not to open up the door and jump out. TUCK AND ROLL!

I'm going to have to tell my son about the birds and the bees in the car on the way to my father's house. I don't even *get* the term, "the birds and the bees". How does that properly teach a kid about sex? You never see a pigeon railing a dove or a honey bee sticking it to a bumble bee. They really need to call it, "the cows and the horses". Just the other day we drove by a farm and one cow was mounted up on another cow and Gavin said, "Awww look, Mommy. That cow is giving the other cow a hug!" I could have explained it easily then. I could have used correct terminology like penis and sperm and fertilization. It was a farm for fuck's sake. That sort of stuff can be seen every two feet between goats and pigs and roosters and chickens. I could have given him plenty of examples. But then I would have to answer the age old question about which came first, the chicken or the egg and that question still boggles MY mind. Now I'm going to have to make up some type of analogy that has to do with phones. "First, you pull the antenna out so it's nice and long, then you push the right buttons so the other phone is in the mood to make a call…"

44

I can't do this. I'm not ready for this. He's too young to know about long distance phone calls and roaming charges!

"M-o-o-o-o-m! Did you hear me? I said I know what you guys are doin' when you make phone calls," Gavin repeats.

Sure, go ahead and repeat it. Obviously you need to make sure we are sufficiently freaked out. CHILDREN ARE THE DEVIL.

Maybe if I just completely ignore the situation, he'll forget about it. I turned on the radio, frantically searching for a song he knows that he can butcher the lyrics to.

Why is there so much fucking talk radio at five o'clock in the evening?

"Ooooh, this is a good song, Gavin! Do you know this song?" I ask overenthusiastically.

Carter looks at me like I'm insane as Kenny G notes filled the car.

Fucking Kenny G. Couldn't you record ONE song with some lyrics? Michael Bolton taught you nothing. Epic fail, Kenny. Epic fail.

"You guys always lock your door when you make phone calls," Gavin says.

Son of a bitch, Kenny G! You put everyone to sleep but my son. The ONE thing you had going for you and now it's gone to shit.

"You guys kiss in there, don't you?" Gavin asks.

I stop swaying to beat of Kenny G and shut off the BIC Lighter App on my phone, noticing that Carter is still looking at me funny. It's like he's never met me. I'm trying to get Gavin's mind off of fertilization and bees fucking pigeons!

"YES!" Carter shouts. "That's *exactly* what we do. We kiss. That's all we do. Just kiss. Sometimes Mommy and Daddy need to lock the door so we can kiss. And...just kiss. What else would we do in there besides kiss? Ha ha! Mommy and Daddy sittin' in a tree, K-I-S-S-"

I reach over and squeeze his arm to get him to stop talking as we pull into my dad's driveway. Gavin unbuckles his seatbelt and scrambles out of the car to race to my dad, his attention already diverted. My dad scoops him up into his arms and meets us at the car as Carter gets Gavin's overnight bag out of the backseat, and I stand by my open door, breathing a sigh of relief that Sex Ed with our four-year-old is finally over.

"Hey, Papa! Mommy and Daddy lock their door so they can kiss!" Gavin tells him excitedly.

My dad looks a little grossed out and quickly changes the subject.

"I got that movie *'Gnomeo and Juliet'* for us to watch tonight," he tells Gavin.

Sadly, Gavin isn't going to be deterred even for garden gnomes that come to life and ass rape a small community while they sleep. I'm sure that's not what really happens in a children's movie, but in my mind it is. Garden gnomes are creepy. I firmly believe they come to life after you go to bed at night and violate you.

"Mommy and Daddy make a lot of noise when they kiss. Mommy talks to God a lot. I talk to God sometimes too. I asked him for a puppy and a new monster truck but I was nice and didn't yell at him like Mommy does. He still hasn't gotten me the puppy though."

And on that note, we kiss Gavin good-bye, jump into the car, and take off. My dad can deal with the birds and the bees and cows and the chickens and the kissing horses while visions of his daughter screaming for Jesus dance in his head.

We pull up to Liz and Jim's house fifteen minutes later and park in the street behind the biggest limo bus I've ever seen. Liz had told me she rented something small and modest to drive us around so we wouldn't have to worry about ruining someone's night and forcing them to be our designated driver. Obviously her version of small and modest differ greatly from mine. This thing could house an entire football team with room to spare.

46

"It's about time you two fuckers got here!" Drew yells as he meets us at the end of the driveway, tossing a beer through the air towards Carter.

In honor of the wine tours that evening, Drew dons a shirt with a picture of a corkscrew on the front that reads, "I pull out."

We walk up the bus steps to join everyone else, noticing they are all well on their way toward getting drunk, everyone except Liz. She is all alone at the very back of the bus with her arms folded and a scowl on her face.

I take one look at her and know I had made it there just in time.

How could this have happened? Why wasn't anyone helping my poor friend?

Leaving Carter at the front of the bus with Drew, Jim, and Jenny, I hurry down the aisle and sit down next to Liz.

"Who did this to you?" I ask angrily as I wrap my arm around her shoulder.

She looks at me and I swear I see her lip quiver.

"It's okay. You can tell me. We'll fix it," I reassure her as I rub soothing circles on her back.

I see hope flare in her eyes, and I know she's going to be fine. I will make this better for her if it's the last thing I do.

"My mother! It was her. It was all her!" she wails in anguish.

I quickly glance to the front of the bus, fearing that just *thinking* about Mrs. Gates will suddenly make her appear. Forget bridezilla! Mrs. Gates is mother-of-the-bridezilla. She is the biggest wedding Nazi in the world. Every single wedding tradition, old wives tale, ritual, and custom, Mary Gates believes in it, practices it, and forces everyone around her to participate in it.

Right now, my poor best friend is wearing a rhinestone tiara with a veil attached, a sash across the front of her that reads, "Bride to Be", and underneath that sash, a tee-shirt with individually wrapped suckers strategically attached directly on top of her boobs. In

47

bright pink glitter puff paint are the words, "Suck for a Buck".

"I'm in bachelorette party hell!" Liz screeches.

I reach over and started plucking suckers off of her boobs.

"It's okay; I'm going to get you out of this," I tell her.

"Claire Donna Morgan, I hope you're giving my daughter a dollar for every one of those suckers you are removing from her shirt!"

It's like something out of a movie. The music that pumps out of the limo's speakers screeches to a halt and all of the laughter from our friends immediately dies.

"Run! Save yourself!" Liz whispers loudly as she tries to shove me away from her.

I slowly stand up and put on a brave face, letting my friend know that I will take one for the team. I will stand in between her and sudden bachelorette party death. I turn around just in time to be bum rushed in the aisle.

"Can you believe my baby is getting married?!" Mrs. Gates squeals as she throws a sash over my head that reads, "Maid-of-Honor" before I can blink.

She pulls me into a tight hug, bouncing me up and down like we're long lost sorority sisters, the cloying scent of White Diamonds perfume surrounding me and threatening to make my eyes water.

Where my family is more along the lines of the Connor family from the show Roseanne, Alice's family leans more toward The Brady Bunch.

On crack.

Or maybe acid.

Which is the one that makes you see fuzzy bunnies singing about lollypops and kittens and puppies frolicking on a rainbow?

"Claire, I am entrusting you to make sure my baby has a great time tonight," Mrs. Gates says sternly as she pulls away from me and thrusts a piece of paper in my hand. "This is a treasure hunt for Liz. You have to make sure she does every single thing on the list

48

before the night is out. I've been told this is all the rage with you young people."

Don't look down at the list; don't look down at the list.

"Well, don't just stand there, Claire. Look at the list!" Mrs. Gates demands excitedly.

"Get a stranger to give you his underwear," I mutter, reading the first line.

Mrs. Gates squeals like little girl. "Oh my gosh this is going to be a hoot! Keep reading!"

I take a deep breath, forcing the vomit that had lodged itself in my throat to remain where it is and not splatter all over the piece of paper in my hand.

On second thought...no list equals no scavenger hunt.

"And don't worry, I made enough copies for everyone!" Liz's mom says enthusiastically as she pulls a handful of papers out of her purse and starts passing them out.

I cover my hand over my mouth as I scan the list. No point in puking now. I'll never be able to projectile vomit far enough to reach all the copies.

Find a guy with an accent.

Meet a guy with the same name as the groom and take a picture with him.

Make out with one of the bridesmaids.

I really don't think I should be sober for this right now.

"Mrs. Gates, you are looking positively radiant this evening. Have I mentioned that yet?" Jim states sweetly as he comes up behind his future mother-in-law and puts his arm around her shoulder.

"Now, don't try and distract me, James. I've got something for you too," she says as she unfolds a baseball hat that said "Groom" on it and places it on his head.

"Folks, if this is everyone, I need you all to take your seats so we can leave," the limo driver informs us as he pokes his head in the door of the bus.

"Well, I guess that's my cue to leave," Mrs. Gates says as she stands there, not making *any* attempt at moving.

She glances around at everyone expectantly, waiting for someone to beg her to stay and join us.

No one speaks.

Or moves. There might have even been an uncomfortable cough that I think came from the driver.

"Okay....well...you kids have fun now!" she finally says as she walks to the door of the bus. "Oh my goodness, I almost forgot the most important thing!"

She turns back around and rushes down the aisle towards Liz. Everyone groans quietly.

Mrs. Gates stops in front of her daughter and reaches into the giant suitcase she calls a purse and pulls out a penis. Or should I say, *"penis products."* Lots and lots of penis products, things I didn't even know they made in the shape of a penis, and now I will have to bleach my eyes at the thought of Liz's mom walking into a store and purchasing these items:

A candy necklace full of sugary penises, a penis-shaped water bottle, a penis-shaped pacifier that she decides needed to be tied around my neck.

Yes, I am absolutely going to stay classy this evening.

But she isn't done yet, oh no. Next out of her bag of tricks: penis-shaped pasta. Seriously? What the fuck do we need with a bag of penis-shaped pasta on a limo bus? We're not going to fill a pan with some water from the tiny bathroom at the back of the bus and stick it on the engine to boil it so we can make maca*weenie* and cheese.

She hands Jenny a box of penis gummies that Drew tells her to open up immediately because he wants to hear her say, "This penis tastes so good." Last but not least, she hands everyone different colored rubber penis pen caps. Because you know, at some point during the night there might be an emergency that calls for someone to write a note using only a pen with a penis pen cap.

I should check the scavenger hunt. It could be on the list.

Mrs. Gates looks like a perverted Mary Poppins pulling penises out of her carpet bag. I'm waiting for her to pull out a penis-shaped lamp or a penis-shaped coat stand. When she finally emptied her bag of all things phallic, she steps off of the bus and we all let out sighs of relief—and then we rip every single sash, hat, veil, and suck for a buck item off of us.

Drew pours everyone a shot of Tequila Rose (in penis shot glasses, of course) and passes them out.

"What is this pussy shit?" Jim asks as he sniffs the thick, pink liquid in his shot glass.

"It smells like strawberry milk," I say with a cringe. I don't know about anyone else, but milk and liquor just does not sound like it should go together.

"It tastes like strawberry milk too. And it's good shit. I thought I'd start us off with something girly tonight so know one hurls in the first hour," Drew explains.

We all nod in understanding. No one wants to be the first one to puke.

The six of us sit at the back of the bus around the semi-circle leather couch. We raise our shot glasses in the air until they all clink together in the middle.

"I'd like to propose a toast," Drew says. "Here's to you, here's to me – fuck you, here's to me!"

We all down the shots as the bus starts up and pulls away from the curb.

6. BACK DOOR ACTION

Oh. My. God. What is that noise? WHAT IS THAT NOISE??

It feels like someone is screaming in my ear with a bullhorn. I let out a groan, roll over, and pull the covers up over my head in an effort to stop it from exploding.

Sweet Jesus what did I do last night?

"CLAIRE! For fuck's sake shut your alarm clock off!"

The yelling from Liz on the other side of my door makes me cringe. I pull the covers down just far enough so I can squint at my alarm clock.

Sure enough, the sound that's threatening to make my ears bleed is coming from that little bastard on our dresser across the room.

The repetitive flash of the time, its bright red numbers, and the staccato beeping on that thing makes me think its judging me. I can hear it— tequila, shots, vodka, karaoke, you're an idiot.

"Carter," I mumble.

Jesus, my voice sounds like I swallowed a bucket full of gravel. It feels that way too.

"Carter," I groan again. "Shut off the alarm clock."

With my squinty eye, I turn my head as slowly as possible and see the spot next to me in bed is empty.

"Shit."

I stick my arm out from under my cocoon and grab the first thing my fingers touch on my nightstand—a vibrator with a leash on it. It's a sad, sad day when something like this doesn't faze me. I whip it across the room and watch the giant pink rubber penis and its diamond-studded leash crash into the alarm clock and effectively shut it up.

Small bursts of memories from last night flash through my addled brain and make me wish I can have a lobotomy.

Did I sing "Like a Virgin" at a winery? And why am I not wearing any underwear?

With my eyes squeezed shut so the bright rays of sun shining through the window don't light them on fire, I stumble out of bed and throw on a pair of yoga pants that are crumpled on the floor. I slowly make my way out of the bedroom and into the living room.

"Yo, Claire Bear! You're alive!" Drew shouts from his spot on the couch as I peel my eyes open and gave him the finger for being so cheerful and not hungover.

How is that possible? He drank way more than me. I think. And why is he in our living room? I'm going to start charging this asshole rent.

I stare at the annoying smile on Drew's face and another memory from last night assaults me as I walk up to the kitchen table and pull out a chair.

"Why do I remember you peeing somewhere in this house?" I ask with my gravelly voice that I hope is just from yelling and singing and not from puking somewhere I can't recall.

"Did you pee on this chair?" I ask angrily as my ass hovers above the seat cushion.

"Yes, he peed in that chair," Liz answers as she emerges from the laundry room off of the kitchen.

"Fuck, it's like we have a puppy," I mutter as I move to take a seat at one of the bar stools by the island instead.

"I didn't pee *that* bad on it," Drew complains as he walks into the kitchen and makes a show of looking really hard at the chair in question.

"There is no GOOD level of pee on a chair, Drew!" I yell as I take the glass of water and aspirin Liz had set down on the counter in front of me. I throw the pills in my mouth and chug the entire glass of water.

I hear the faint sound of music coming from somewhere and realize my purse is singing the theme song from "Golden Girls". Liz and Drew start cracking

53

up behind me as I reach to the end of the island and grab my purse, realizing by their snickers that one of them must have changed my ring tone.

I dig through my purse trying to find the damn phone before that fucking song is stuck in my head all day.

"......traveled down the road and back again. Your heart is true; you're a pal and a confidant..."

My hand finally wraps around the offending cell phone and I quickly hit the send button to stop the song before I even get it out of my purse.

"Hello?" I turn around to glare at Liz and Drew, mouthing the words *"What the fuck?"* to them silently as I answer the phone. That just causes them to laugh even harder.

"Wow, I didn't think you'd be awake yet after last night."

The sound of Carter's voice makes me forget that my so-called friends put some stupid ass song on my phone that I won't be able to stop humming now.

"Did we have sex last night?" I ask, having no shame whatsoever in the fact that I don't remember. Generally, I like to know why I wake up with no pants or underwear on. It's just a little quirk I have.

"Are you referring to before or after we got home?" he asks.

"Uh, both?"

Carter sighs. "I don't think you're awake or sober enough to discuss the sex we had before we got home. After...well, I do believe sex was the general idea until I got your clothes off and you puked on me."

"Ooooh, sorry about that," I apologize sheepishly.

"It's my fault. I should have never introduced you to Drew," he replies jokingly.

"He peed on our chair," I complain, giving Drew the two-finger eye salute.

"You puked on my dick," Carter deadpans.

"Fine, you win," I say with a sigh. "So where are you?"

"DUDE! LET ME TELL HER ABOUT THE BACK DOOR ACTION ON THE BUS!" Drew yells into the phone as he comes up next to me.

I turn to look at Drew with a horrified look on my face.

"What are you talking about?" I ask him. "Carter, what the fuck is he talking about?" I screech into the phone. "Oh Jesus. Did I let you...did we...OH MY GOD WE DID THAT ON A BUS SURROUNDED BY OUR FRIENDS?"

The laughter comes from all around me now. Liz bends over so far in hysterics that she's fallen on the floor; Drew wipes tears out of his eyes as he leans against the counter, and Carter was snorting on the other end of the phone.

"No! No, it's not what you're thinking. Even though you begged me repeatedly saying, 'Come on just stick it in my ass!' I figured that was not a decision you were making with one hundred percent clarity. Tell me you at least remember being in the bathroom with me," Carter begs.

I put my elbows up on the counter and lean my head against one hand, closing my eyes to try and conjure up the bathroom rendezvous Carter speaks of.

Everyone piles back on the bus after the third winery, a little louder and a lot drunker. Carter slumps onto the leather bench, pulling me down next to him until I am practically sprawled on top of him with my chest resting against his. He holds my face in both of his hands, and as the bus starts moving and our friends start yelling and goofing off in the front of the vehicle, he leans in and kissed me. His tongue slowly pushes past my lips and sweeps through my mouth causing butterflies to erupt in the pit of my stomach and warmth to spread between my legs. After a few minutes he pulls his mouth away from mine, and I let out a groan at the loss.

"You wanna go in the bathroom?" Carter asks with a wag of his eyebrows.

"No. I don't have to pee right now," I tell him as I leaned toward him so I can kiss him again. He tastes so yummy, like wine and sunshine and kittens.

"I'm not talking about going to the bathroom to GO to the bathroom. I'm talking about going to the bathroom so I can stick it to you," he says with a snort and a laugh.

"You're so romantic. Say it again," I tell him as I bat my eyelashes at him.

Carter looks over my shoulder and then back down at me.

"Seriously. No one is looking. We could sneak into the bathroom and no one would even know. I'll make it quick."

"No really, keep going. This is totally turning me on," I tell him in a monotone voice.

Carter pulls my face back toward him and our lips crash together. His tongue skates over my bottom lip before plunging back into my mouth. The pain of the week-long exiles while we work opposite shifts have become glaringly obvious as we deepened the kiss, and I practically crawl onto his lap.

Carter's hand slides down the side of my body, brushing over one breast and curving over my hip to clutch my ass and pull me closer to him. He moves his mouth away from my lips and starts planting warm, wet, open-mouthed kisses along my neck and collarbone until I feel like I'll melt into a puddle of goo on the floor of the bus. He gently grazes the side of my neck with his teeth and slides his tongue over the spot. I'm panting like a dog at this point and know I won't make it much longer. If he keeps this up, I'm going to throw him down on the seat and bang him in front of everyone.

"Okay, fine. You win. Bathroom. Now," I mumble through my drunken, lust-induced haze.

We stand up quickly and stumble our way to the tiny bathroom directly across from us. I vaguely hear one of the girls shout, "NO, no, no! I have to pee!" before we slam the door closed and fumble with the sliding lock. The bathroom is about the size of an

56

airplane bathroom so maneuverability is nil. Carter's body is pressed up against my back and he begins kissing and sucking on the back of my neck as I try in vain to get the stupid lock to slide closed.

"I can't get the fucking door to lock!" I complain through moans of pleasure as he brings his hands around my waist and slides them up my body until they cup both of my breasts.

"Fuck it. I think it locks automatically anyway. That slide thing is just for the little sign on the outside that switches to 'occupied' or some shit. Everyone already knows we're in here," Carter says as he starts massaging my breasts.

We turn as one so I can rest my hands on the edge of the sink and Carter can lift my skirt. A quick breaking of the bus makes me jerk forward and slam my shoulder into the wall above the sink.

"Son of a bitch!" I yell. "This is going to be dangerous."

I giggle as Carter slides his hands back down my sides and grazes over a particularly ticklish spot.

"You're not supposed to be laughing. This is supposed to be awesome and hot," he states as his hands slide down my thighs and then immediately back up, pushing my skirt up to my hips as he went.

"Oh believe me, it's totally hot," I say with another giggle as the bus takes off and we fall backwards. Carter falls on top of the toilet, and I landed on his lap with an "oooomph".

"Okay, this might not have been one of our best ideas," I say with a laugh as I try to get up but the bus takes a curve and we both crash our shoulders into the wall on the left right beneath the little bathroom window.

"Dammit! We WILL have sex in this thing if it kills us," Carter states as he pushes me off of his lap and stands back up behind me.

"Carter, I think this IS going to kill us. My dad is going to have to tell his friends that his daughter died in a limo bus bathroom with her skirt up around her hips. That is not okay!"

The bus straightens and maintains a steady, non-deadly speed and a quick glance out of the window shows us that we were on a long stretch of highway.

"Are you sure no one can see us in here?" I ask in a panic as I feel Carter's hands slide up the back of my thighs and then pull my underwear down a few inches.

I hear his zipper open and fabric rustling and before I can think of any other reasons why this isn't such a great idea, one of his hands slide around to the front, between my legs, and his fingers slide through my wetness. I had been aching with need for him since he first put his hand on my bare thigh in the car earlier. Having him touch me like this, for the first time in a week, makes me throw all rationale out the window - where I am pretty certain no one could see us.

"No one can see us," he whispers against my neck, practically reading my mind as two of his fingers plunge inside of me, and he slides his smooth, hardness between the cheeks of my ass. "The window in here is made of special glass. When you shut the door, it hits a trigger so we can see out, but no one can see in. Jim told me about it earlier."

He continues to slide his fingers in and out of me in a slow, tortuous fashion and like he wasn't just talking about the sexual safety features on the bus.

"Holy hell," I moan as he pulls his two fingers up to circle my clit.

I think I hear horns honking and shouts coming from outside but at that point I don't really care if we are stopped in a rest area and people are eating popcorn while staring in the window.

"Fuck, I need you," I tell him as I let go of the sink with one hand and reach back to grab onto his hip and pull him harder against me. "You should TOTALLY give me 'nother baby," I murmur drunkenly.

Carter laughs as he pulls a condom out of the back pocket of his jeans and rips open the foil with his teeth.

"I'm pretty sure you don't really mean that," he says as I feel his hands graze my ass while he sheathes himself.

"Who cares if I mean it? The wine and vodka mean it. And they are ALWAYS serious. Give me your seeeeeeed."

I snort and blink my eyes a few times to get the room to stop spinning.

Carter places both of his hands on my hips and I feel the tip of his penis at my opening. I let out a loud moan and Carter quickly reaches up and puts his hand over my mouth with a laugh.

"Not so loud, baby. Everyone will hear you."

I pull Carter's hand off of my mouth long enough to spout even more nonsense as he slowly pushes himself inside me.

"You should stick it in my ass."

"I am not going to stick it in your ass," Carter says with a muted groan as he moves a little deeper.

"Come on, you know you want to stick it in my ass," I goad him loudly.

His hand comes back up to cover my mouth and my laughter turns into a pleasure-filled whimper as he pushes all the way inside me and holds himself still.

"You should know that as a guy, I am pre-programmed to always want to stick it in your ass. I hope tomorrow you will appreciate my self control," Carter explains as he slowly starts moving inside me.

"If you knock on my backdoor right now, I will totally let you in," I giggle.

Carter stops again and takes a couple of deep calming breaths.

"Careful back there, though, there's a rickety step. Don't fall in my backdoor."

Carter tries not to laugh as he begins thrusting harder, forcing my hips to bump against the edge of the sink. Thoughts of sperm and the porch by my backdoor flow out of my mind.

"Fuck, why did you have to start talking about sticking it in your ass? I'm not going to be able to last long," he complains as he tries to slow down.

59

"Just shut up and keep going. I'm too drunk to care right now, and you should appreciate that shit!" I yell around his hand that's still held against my mouth.

The faint sounds of horns honking still make their way into my brain as he curses and moves faster against me, his orgasm barreling through him like a freight train.

His hand drops from my mouth and he braces his arms on either side of mine on the edge of the sink as he buries his head in the side of my neck. He comes with a muffled shout and I grip the sink tighter so we won't topple over.

We stood there breathing heavy for a few minutes before he pulls himself out of me and we right our clothes. He gives me a quick kiss and promises me five of my very own orgasms in repayment before we open the door and walk out into the aisle of the bus.

All of our friends are standing there cheering and clapping, and it was then that we noticed the bus was stopped and a police officer was standing behind them with his arms crossed in front of him.

"Oh my God, we got arrested?" I ask Carter.

Why the fuck don't I remember going to jail? Was I somebody's bitch now?

"No," he laughs. "We just got a ticket for indecent exposure. Turns out Jim didn't explain the bathroom door situation clearly. That little lever you were trying to slide over? THAT'S what blacks out the window so no one can see in. Oops."

Drew starts laughing and I noticed that he inches close enough to me so he can put his ear right next to mine and hear Carter's end of the conversation I shove him away when I realize that's what he was doing.

"Ha ha get it, Claire? Back door action? I was talking about the bathroom door. Or was I talking about you shouting for Carter to fuck you in the ass over and over? Hmmm, I'm not sure. They are equally entertaining to think about," Drew says with a laugh.

Oh my God. This day can't get any worse.

60

"So anyway, I was just calling to make sure you were alive. As you can see, everyone ended up crashing at our place since the bus stopped there first. Jim gave Jenny a ride home this morning to take a shower and left Liz and Drew behind to make sure you didn't choke on your own vomit or anything. I'm on my way to pick Gavin up from your dad's and then we're meeting my parents for brunch. There's been a slight change of plans. Instead of them coming to our house, they rented out the small party room at the Oberlin Inn where they're staying. They wanted to invite your dad, Drew, Jenny, Liz, and Jim and they didn't want to impose on us."

I quickly say good-bye to Carter and kick Liz and Drew out of the house so I can take a shower and start to feel a little more human.

Hopefully, that will be the extent of my embarrassing behavior from last night.

7. WHORE DIZZLE

I shower, dress and walk through the lobby of the Oberlin Inn in record time. I no longer reek of stale liquor, but I'm pretty sure I still look like ass. A view of my reflection in a mirror behind the registration desk confirms my suspicions.

"Mommy, you look old today," Gavin says as we walk hand in hand around the corner and down the hall. "Like old lady and eye balls."

"Gee, thanks. I love you too," I mumble.

Carter had got a call to come into work to fill out a form that will add Gavin to his health benefits, so after he picked Gavin up from my dad's and dropped him back off with me, he ran up there and said he would meet us at the inn.

Yeah, that's exactly what I want to do. Walk into the lion's den alone.

I had made a quick call to Drew and Jenny and asked if I could pick them up on the way for moral support. I've spoken to Carter's parents a few times on the phone since we moved in together, but this will be the first time they actually see me and meet Gavin. I am beyond nervous about making a good impression. They are the complete opposite from what I'm used to. They never swear, they only drink on special occasions, and I'm pretty sure they've never puked in anyone's lap after a night out bar hopping. I figured since Mr. and Mrs. Ellis already know Drew and haven't forbid Carter from hanging out with him yet, I should be okay.

"I still can't believe you don't remember screaming at that old lady in the parking lot. It was priceless!" Drew whispers from behind me as we walk into the party room and see Carter and his parents talking to a waiter.

"I'm so glad I downloaded the theme from "Golden Girls" to her phone right after that occurred," Jenny says to Drew.

"It really was a stroke of brilliance," he replies.

I roll my eyes and try not to think about the events from last night that Drew and Jenny regaled me with on the ride over. Some things are best left forgotten—or lost in a drunken haze that no one should ever speak of again.

As we walk through the doorway of the room, Carter turns and we make eye contact. I suddenly don't want to kill the two people behind me. Everything is momentarily forgotten when I look at him.

I can do this. Parents love me.

He excuses himself from the discussion and hurries over to us, scooping Gavin up in his arms and peppering his face with kisses. He reaches out and grabbed my hand to pull me in close and place a soft kiss on my lips.

"Mmmmm. You don't taste like vomit and desperation anymore," he whispers with a smirk as he pulls his face away from mine.

"Remind me to never drunk dial you again for a booty call," I reply with mock irritation.

"Don't worry," he says as he turns and pulls me over to his parents. "If that's your idea of a booty call, I'm never taking another call from you again at two in the morning from the kitchen while you're down the hall in the bedroom. My penis can't handle another rejection like that. Or should I say *projection?*"

Drew and Jenny start giggling behind us.

"Alright, get it all out of your system now you guys. We are never, ever speaking of what happened last night again. We all need to pretend like it never happened," I state firmly as Carter wraps his arm around my waist and hefts Gavin up higher.

"Yeah, about that," Drew says sheepishly, "you might want to check Facebook when you get a free moment."

My mouth dropped open, and I could do nothing but stare at his back as he pushes us out of the way and drags Jenny up to greet Madelyn and Charles and give them a hug. I barely paid attention as Drew introduces Jenny to them. Before I know it, all eyes are on me and Gavin.

"Say hello to your grandparents, Gavin," Carter prompts him.

"Hi, I'm Gavin. When I'm ten I can drink beer and mow the lawn," he states with a smile.

Nothing like a little tension breaker.

"Well, isn't that sweet," Madelyn says in a voice that clearly states it's anything but.

"It's good to finally meet you Clarissa," Charles says distractedly as he stares at Jenny's ass when she bends over to pick up her lip gloss that she had dropped.

"Dad, it's *Claire*," Carter reminds him in a low voice, giving me an apologetic look.

As Gavin and I are pulled in for impolite hugs and air kisses, all I can do is try and think about what I may or may not have put on Facebook. The fact that I am pretty sure Carter's mother hated me on sight and his father is too busy ogling my friend's assets to get my name right doesn't even touch a nerve. If I had put a picture of my boobs on Facebook, I'd throw myself off of a bridge anyway, so their judgments won't matter.

Under normal circumstances, I own who I am. I like to have fun and go crazy, occasionally, and when that happens, it usually involves alcohol. I don't drink and drive and I don't spend my money on hookers and crack. I don't waste my paycheck every week filling up entire shopping carts with bottles of Jack like Nicolas Cage in *Leaving Las Vegas*, and sometimes my shenanigans are broadcast on Facebook either by my own stupidity or by the stupidity of my friends. Typically, this is only slightly embarrassing, and we would all have a good laugh over it for months to come. However, in a moment of insanity a few days ago, I had decided to friend-request Carter's mother and a few other members of his family on Facebook. I really should be supervised anytime I go near social media. There should be an actual human being whose only job is to sit next to me and say things like, "Do NOT post that," and "You should seriously consider removing your tag off of that picture," or "No, dick does not

64

rhyme with delicious, and you are not good at poetry when you're drunk, contrary to what you've been told," and "That comment sounds a lot better in your head than it will under her picture. And that's not how you spell cock sucking whore anyway".

After we conclude a few minutes of small talk, Madelyn and Charles whisk Gavin away and begin spoiling him by letting him order anything he wants on the menu, even if it's five different desserts. I turn to glare at Drew as Carter moves behind me and wraps his arms around my waist.

"Why the hell do I need to check Facebook?" I practically screech at him. "What did you let me do?"

"Well, the word 'vagina' may have been used in several posts last night," Drew informs me seriously. "As well as a few words even *I've* never heard before."

I can feel Carter's rumble of laughter as his chest presses up against my back.

"Oh this should be good," he says absently as he rests his chin on my head.

I shake my head in denial, completely horrified at the fact that I drunk Facebooked last night.

How can he be so calm? God only knows what I did that his mother might have seen.

"No wonder your mother isn't very impressed by me," I state.

"Nah, don't take that personally. Madelyn Ellis was born with a stick up her ass," Drew reassures me.

"It's true, she was," Carter agreed. "And they love you so stop it."

A few minutes later, Liz, Jim, and my father arrive and after introducing themselves to Carter's parents, they make their way over to our little group.

"So, I'm guessing since you're still alive Carter's mom either hasn't read her Facebook page yet or she has a really good sense of humor," Liz says with a laugh.

Oh my God. That's it! I'm putting an ad out for new friends.

"I should have been nowhere even remotely near Facebook in that condition. What is wrong with you people?!" I yell in a loud whisper so Carter's parents won't hear my hysterical breakdown from their table over by the kitchen where they are currently showing Gavin what each utensil is for and how to place the napkin in his lap.

Oh Jesus. They have manners. They have manners and they're all proper and know which fork to use, and I took a dump on their Facebook page last night.

"You guys let her near the internet when you went out? Jim should especially know better. How many times has she lifted your cell phone and hacked your Facebook page to tell everyone you like to eat baked beans off of hookers?" My dad asks with a chuckle.

"I wouldn't laugh if I were you, George. I remember when she changed your status to say, 'Can anyone tell me what it means when your penis has a blue discharge that smells like egg salad?'" Jim reminds him.

"So who let the dip shit near a phone?" my dad questions.

Can you feel the love? Can you? It feels almost like having my toenails ripped out.

"Well, at first we thought we should take her Blackberry away for her own safety and for that of those around her. But when she posted, "Spitters are quitters" on every one of Carter's cousin's pictures in her photo album, at that point it was just too funny to put a stop to." Drew laughs.

Oh fuck me.

I vaguely remember while Carter was up at the bar buying a bottle of wine at the fourth winery, I told everyone the story about how his cousin Katie gave some guy a blow job in college and gagged on his spunk. The very same story she had just told me a few days ago when she accepted my friend request and swore me to secrecy. Yes, I realize this is very personal information to be sharing with an almost-stranger, but we bonded quickly over Facebook email, what can I say? I may have suggested that if I told anyone her deep, dark secret she could shave my head.

Double fuck.

"I really don't want to hear the story about my cousin that goes along with that, do I?" Carter asks as I crane my neck around to see the grimace on his face.

"Probably not," I mutter as I look back at Liz.

"Give me your phone. Now," I state with my hand out to her.

Of course, today of all days my phone's battery is dead and I've left the fucking thing at home.

Liz pulls her iPhone out of her purse and slaps it into my open palm. I yanked it to me faster than a fat kid with a piece of cake and quickly click on the Facebook icon and log into my account.

"Holy fucking shit," I whisper as the little globe symbol at the top of the screen tells me I have sixty-five new notifications.

Liz moves over next to me and glances over my shoulder.

"Oh don't worry. Most of those were you replying to your own posts using my account. You were really cracking yourself up last night."

This is doing nothing to make me feel better. I go to Katie's page and clicked on one of the two photo albums she had in there. I quickly scan through the pictures and don't find any offending comments. Maybe I had deleted them.

Right, and maybe fairies will start shitting money on my front lawn.

"Wrong photo album," Drew states as he also comes around behind me so he can peer over my other shoulder. "The photo album you want is the one titled, *'Missionary Trip to Jerusalem.'* And yes, I totally just said 'missionary' without laughing."

I am going straight to hell.

At this point, Carter moves his head to the side, right next to mine, so he too can look down at the phone.

I click on the correct album and sure enough, under every single photo from her trip to Jerusalem with people from her CHURCH GROUP, I have posted the words, "Spitters are quitters."

"Oooh, oooh, wait! This is my favorite part!" Drew says excitedly as he snatches the phone out of my hand and navigates to the last picture in the album.

He finds what he was looking for and barks out a laugh before handing the phone back to me. I grab it out of his hand roughly and shoot him a dirty look for his excitement at my epic fail.

Not only does it say "Spitters are quitters" under the last photo in the album, but below that stellar use of the English language I have written, "Jesus is my homeboy."

"Your cousin is never going to forgive me," I said with a sigh.

"Eh, she's a bitch anyway. Someone needed to put her in her place." Carter laughs as he tightens his hold on me.

I reach my arm out to hand the phone back to Liz and notice a funny look on her face.

"What?" I ask with trepidation, my arm just hanging there since she hadn't reached out to take the phone from me.

"Oh fuck, there's more?" I question her as my shoulders drooped.

"You might want to take a gander at the conversation we had on Carter's mom's page," she says, not even bothering to contain the laughter at this point.

I'm sure my eyes are the size of dinner plates as I just stand there staring at her.

"Oh my God! I forgot about that! I read it again this morning and almost pissed myself!" Drew chuckles. "Not on any furniture," he says to me in total seriousness.

I regretfully bring the phone back to me and pull Madelyn Ellis' Facebook page up.

At exactly 12:28 a.m. I had posted the following on Madelyn's page:

"You are a gigantic, stinkotic, vaginastic, clitoral, liptistic whore dizzle."

Three minutes later Liz responds with: *"Dude, was this meant for me? You just posted this on Carter's mom's page. Ha! You dumb ass!"*

I stare at the rest of the conversation, ON CARTER'S MOM'S PAGE, and I want to vomit. His MOM'S page, people! I don't think you understand the level of suck we're at right now.

Claire Morgan: *You are a furry nut sack on the giant dick of my life.*

Elizabeth Gates: *You are the taco to my furry heart.*

Claire Morgan: *Where is your Dumbo-earred vagina? I can hear it flapping from here. Are you trying to fly back to me?*

Elizabeth Gates: *My vagina is way nicer than anything you own you drizzly, weighted down orca of a woman.*

Claire Morgan: *Your vagina is like a burning clown car...this flaming taco with hundreds of screaming people trying get the fuck out of it.*

Elizabeth Gates: *Dumb shit whore.*

Claire Morgan: *Dick weed.*

By the time I got to the bottom of the thread, Carter has stepped away from me and is practically convulsing with laughter.

Carter's parents choose that moment to walk Gavin back over to us, and I am praying to God, Allah, Buddha, and Ryan Seacrest that she had not logged into her Facebook account yet today so I can get in there and delete everything.

Drew and Jim are now huddled together behind me quoting those posts back and forth to each other in loud whispers and laughing like hyenas.

"Claire, you have raised quite the charming young man," Madelyn says with a kind smile. "Gavin is just so precious, and Carter's father and I just want to thank you for taking such good care of our grandson"

Fuck, why does she have to be so nice? She's like a sweet, Disney princess and I'm Girls Gone Wild on crack.

"Right, Charles?"

When he doesn't answer her immediately, she elbows him in the side and he jerks his head back around, no doubt from checking out the waitress.

"Oh, yes. Absolutely, Candy. Wonderful job."

Now it's Candy? Do I look like a fucking stripper?

"Thank you, that means a lot to me," I tell her, pasting on a smile.

"You're looking a little tired today, Claire. Did my son keep you out late last night?" she asks.

Carter tries to cover up a snort from behind me, and my elbow meets his stomach, much in the same way his mother's just had with his father.

I'm pretty sure his mom doesn't want me to tell her my late night involved sex in public, back door begging, sperm demanding, wine drinking debauchery. Although with my luck, those things could be somewhere on Facebook and she'll find out soon enough.

Someone calls Madelyn's name and while she looks away, I pull Liz's phone out from behind my back and furiously pull Facebook back up so I can begin the deletion process. Before I can even get to Madelyn's page, the phone is seized from me.

"Ah-ah-ah! This is a no cell phone zone! And we have a surprise for both of you," Madelyn exclaims with a huge smile as she drops Liz's phone in the front pocket of her dress pants and I try not to whimper. "I'll be right back with your surprise."

She quickly turns and walks away from us, her heels clicking on the wood floor as she exits the party room.

"She's probably going to get her gun. At least she's giving you a head start," my dad whispers.

Carter's father stays with our group and attempts to start up a conversation with my dad while I try to figure out a way to sneak my hand into Madelyn's pants pocket when she comes back without her thinking I'm trying to get to second base.

70

My dad looks blankly at Charles while he yammers on and on about the stock market and their last vacation to France. The first time he had smacked my dad on the arm trying to be all buddy-buddy with him, I feared for Charles', life. My dad looks down at the spot where Charles' hand connected and then back up at him before walking away without another word. Charles doesn't seem phased by it since Liz bends over the table to set her purse down right then and he has something else to occupy his mind.

Drew and Jim are in a deep discussion about having another bachelor party, this time with strippers, when Liz suddenly latches tightly onto my arm and jerks me towards her.

"Oh my God! Who is that?" she whispers in horror as Carter and I turn to see who she is pointing at.

"That's my grandmother," Carter replied with a huge smile as we watch his mom escort an older version of herself into the room. "This must be our surprise. I had no idea she was going to be in town."

At that moment, Drew turns around and spits out the mouthful of water he was drinking. Something about the woman is a little familiar, but I have never met Carter's grandmother. He talks about her all the time and I know that Carter's mother does whatever she asks. Thank God she doesn't do Facebook, at least I don't have *that* to worry about. She'd tell Madelyn to put a hit out on me.

By now, Drew is bent over at the waist with his hands on his knees choking on the water he managed to swallow, and I'm wondering what the fuck his problem is. Jenny smacks him on the back and is making weird head gestures at me and Carter's grandmother like she has some sort of neck tick.

What the hell is going on with everyone?

I'm clearly looking at her with annoyance and put my hands up in the air in a "what the fuck?" gesture. She opens her mouth but before she can say anything, Liz grabs onto my arm with both hands now and is trying to drag me away from everyone. She's alternating between giggles and repeatedly whispering,

71

"Oh sweet Jesus." I'm starting to wonder if everyone around me has been roofied.

I yank my arm out of her clutches and turn around, coming face-to-face with Carter's grandmother. I put a big smile on my face and began to introduce myself when she cuts me off.

"You," is all she says as she looks me up and down.

The look in her eyes and the tilt of her head as she scrutinizes me suddenly forces a memory from last night to surface from the depths of my subconscious.

"She's going to take our cab. Are you kidding me with this shit?" Drew yells indignantly. "I've been standing here trying to hail a cab for like three years and this skank just waltzes in and takes the one that stopped for us."

"Dude, we came in a limo bus. It's parked over there," Jim tells him.

"I don't care if we came here on a magic carpet. That was OUR cab!" I pipe up indignantly.

I stumble over to the back door of the taxi that is still open while the old woman gets situated and stick my head in.

"You're a dick. Go fuck your face," I yell drunkenly before I'm yanked back out by my friends so my head doesn't get mangled by the shutting of the door.

"Dude, you just say that to a seventy-year-old woman!" Drew yells while patting me on the back.

And here that seventy-year-old woman stands with a cocky smile on her face when she sees that I have made the connection to who she is.

The entire room is silent as they watch the exchange between us. I look horrified and Carter's grandmother looks like she's going to throw her little arthritic fists of fury in the air and beat my ass.

There will never ever be another moment in my entire life that is more embarrassing than this one right here. Mark my words.

Madelyn interrupts the stare-down Grandma is giving me, and I suddenly wish there was a hole in the floor that would swallow me up when I see Liz's cell phone in her hand.

"What does 'gigantic, stinkotic, vaginastic, clitoral, liptistic whore dizzle' mean?"

8. THE INCREDIBLE SHRINKING PENIS

"No, Drew, a trip to the strip club will not make everything better," I say for the third time. "Claire is completely mortified after brunch last weekend and thinks my family hates her. She's also pissed at me because according to her, my number one rule as her boyfriend is to stop her from doing anything remotely stupid while she's drunk."

I let out a huge sigh and lift my arms in a "T" so the store owner could measure the length of my chest. While the girls are over with Liz getting a last minute fitting for their dresses, I meet the guys across the street at the mall with Gavin so we can get measured for our tuxes. This might come as a shock, but I've never been measured for a tux or a suit before. When I tell you this is the most awkward moment you will ever have with another person, I'm not lying. It's right up there with prostate exams.

Some strange man named Steve who barely mutters a greeting when we walk in, immediately pushes me in front of a set of mirrors and then gets down on his knees and sticks his hands in the general vicinity of my balls.

Where exactly are you supposed to look when there is a man between your legs cupping your nut sack and he isn't a doctor asking you to bend over and cough? His head? Deep into his eyes when he glances up at you to yell at you for squirming? I'm sorry but I can't stand still when there is all this unwelcome ball-handling going on.

I really don't see why it's necessary to take four measurements that go from where my balls hang to my ankles. My balls haven't moved; you're going to get the same number each time so just write the fucking number down and move on - preferably to a spot away from my nuggets.

Is a store owner even qualified to do this shit? Doesn't he need some type of degree or something before he can just go off wielding a measuring tape and sticking pins in people?

I glance over at Drew and he is looking up at the ceiling and whistling like it's no big deal, like he always has strange people with their hands all over him while they are eye-level with his junk. Wait, look who I'm talking about! It probably had just happened to him at the gas station a half hour before we got here.

"Claire needs to chill. If your parents don't hate *me* by now, they don't hate her. I've done much worse things to them over the years, believe me," Drew says.

"Yeah. I know. My mom still brings up what you did to her parakeet back in high school."

Drew rolls his eyes.

"That wasn't even my fault."

"Uh, you opened the cage and it flew straight into the glass door and died," I remind him.

"Is it my fault that thing was stupid?" he argues. "I thought it would just fly around the room, maybe shit on the carpet. How was I supposed to know it was suicidal? It's your mom's fault really. She should have known her bird was depressed. And frankly, what I did to her Mynah bird was way worse."

Steve spends a few minutes pinning the legs of my pants and gives me a reprieve from ball cupping.

"That bird is *still* saying 'Where my ho's at, bitch?' whenever my dad whistles. My mom couldn't get the bird to stop so she put a ban on whistling in the house," I tell him.

"I really thought she'd be more pissed about the 'Jesus loves me' one. It was just boring every time your mom said that and it replied, 'This I know.' 'Jesus loves me, *fuck a ho'* is much more entertaining," Drew explains.

The person measuring him tells him to turn around so his back is to me.

"Anyway, back to the subject of strippers," he yells over his shoulder. "You are drastically underestimating the power of naked women dancing on poles. That shit could cure cancer or put an end to war

75

if people would open their eyes. Give pole dancers a chance!" Drew shouts with a fist in the air.

"I think you mean 'Give peace a chance.' And watching strange women gyrate on stage is not going to make Claire *less* angry with me. I'm pretty sure that is the exact definition of something that is guaranteed to piss off your girlfriend," I tell him, flinching when a measuring tape is spread across my ass and then as hands glide up and down my legs.

My penis is shrinking. *MY PENIS IS SHRINKING!*

"Sylvia, come here and make sure you have everything you need," the owner yells in the general direction of the back storage room as he stands up and wipes his hands on the front of his pants like being in that close proximity to my manhood made him feel dirty. Shouldn't it be the other way around? I feel violated. I'M THE VICTIM HERE. I just want a tux, not go to second base with Steve, the handsy man who sews.

"I think I have what she needs," Drew leans in and whispers conspiratorially. I glanced up to see a blonde Amazon with a measuring tape draped around her neck walking towards us. You're probably thinking, "Okay, he has nothing to complain about now. Some hot chick is going to get on her hands and knees and touch him!"

False.

Sylvia the Seamstress is stalking towards me, and I suddenly realize just how many people are in this store with nothing better to do than stare at me while they wait for their turn. The lights shining down from above are making me hot and now that I know everyone is watching me, I'm getting the ball sweats. I want to pull the dress pants and my boxers away from my junk but I have to just stand here like an idiot with my arms out to the side because Sylvia is already in front of me...on her knees...reaching for my penis.

I know she's not actually reaching for my penis, but my penis doesn't know that. He's a simple creature and all he knows is that there is a hot woman assuming the position and reaching for him.

I know this is going to be hard for you to comprehend, my friend, but this does not mean she wants to have sex with us. I know it's crazy. I know it doesn't make sense but there it is. Stay strong little buddy, stay strong.

Stop judging me. All men talk to their penises.

Wait! Is the plural of penis, penises? Or is it like the word deer and it's just penis? I have five penis. No, that's not right. Maybe it's peni, long "I" like, "There are too many peni in this porno."

"Could you stand still please?" Sylvia says in an irritated voice.

If she had sweaty balls and an almost-boner she wouldn't be so judgmental. Am I right, or am I right?

"Gavin, you almost dressed?" I call into the dressing room, momentarily forgoing my penis grammar lesson to realize my son had gone in there ten minutes ago, claiming he was a big boy and didn't need any help trying on his tux. I begin to wonder about the brilliance of that decision when I don't hear a reply. Part of me secretly hopes he lit something on fire in there so we can finally put an end to this trauma. At least it forces Sylvia to finish the hell up and move on to the next victim so I can stop giving my penis pep talks.

"Gavin, are you okay in there?" I yell as I take a few steps in that direction. Gavin steps out of the room then in a crisp, brand new toddler tuxedo. Lucky little shit doesn't have to worry about Sylvia or touchy-feely Steve. The suit fits him to perfection and I have to say, he is one handsome little boy.

"Wow, Gav. That looks really good on you," I tell him as I squat down in front of him and fix the buttons he fastened wrong.

"I know. I'm a bad ass, man," he replies as he turns away from me and looks at himself in the mirror. He holds onto the lapels of the suit coat like he is James Bond the Toddler Years and twists from right to left to get a better look.

"Gavin, don't talk like that," I scold.

"Nice suit, little dude," Drew says as he walks up behind Gavin and ruffles his hair. "Mine looks better though."

Gavin turns around and looks up at Drew with an angry look on his face.

"I'm going to put corn and hot sauce on your wiener, and then I'll hit you in the face with it. Hit you in the face with your corny wiener."

"Dude, you are an angry little man," Drew tells him as he shakes his head.

"You're a juice bag!" Gavin yells.

"Okay, time-out. Both of you. Gavin, go put your other clothes back on."

Gavin sticks his tongue out at Drew and turns to run back into the dressing room. I stand up to face Drew and fold my arms in front of me.

"What? He threatened my wiener. He's lucky I didn't throw down fisticuffs with him. And just because he said 'juice bag' doesn't mean we don't both know what he was really thinking. That kid is an evil, evil genius, and I never want to be left alone with him. So, strip club, yea or nay?"

~

"It needs to be tomantic...tmotmantic...ramtantic...dude, it needs to be all loving and shit," Jim states as he goes to sit down next to me on the couch, missing the cushions by about six inches and landing on his ass on the floor.

After all of the fittings are over, the girls take Gavin up to the shop so they can help Claire with some last minute orders, and Drew and Jim decide to stick around our place until they are done. Somehow the topic of my proposal to Claire is brought up and after rehashing the debacle from the Indians game, we all need copious amounts of liquor.

Since Drew's proposal during a ball game idea has gone straight to the shitter, Jim decides it is his turn to try and make this thing work.

"WHY IS THERE A DR. SEUSS CONTACT IN MY CELL PHONE?" Drew yells from his spot sitting Indian-style in the middle of our kitchen table.

"You need candles and you need a violin and you need your shoes shined and a guy in a tux with a white towel thing over his arm and OOHHHH! You need a piano. Chicks dig a guy that can play piano. Can you play the piano, Carter?" Jim asks, finding his way back up to the couch and sprawling across the cushions, kicking me repeatedly in the process.

"Yes! I can play the piano!" I shout.

Why am I shouting?

"I'm not talking about your little Casio keyboard where all you have to do is press the "demo" button and then pretend you're really a piano prodigy," Jim says with a roll of his eyes.

"Whatever, asshole. I can fake-play the SHIT out of "Cherish the Love" by Kool and the Gang. You don't even know. You DON'T. EVEN. KNOW."

I rest my head on the back of the couch and stare up at the ceiling wondering why it's moving.

Ceilings shouldn't move, should they? If ceilings moved, floors would be moving. We'd never be still like broccoli. We'd constantly be moving like in a funhouse. Funhouses are creepy. Funhouses have clowns. Clowns are always moving because they're out to get you and eat your face while you sleep. I wonder if a moving ceiling could kill a clown.

"I DON'T EVEN FUCKING LIKE GREEN EGGS!" Drew shouts from the kitchen, still staring at his phone in anger.

"On my keyboard I used to know how to play "London Bridge is Falling Down" and "Chop Suey".

Heh heh. I said Chop Suey when I meant Chopsticks.

"Chop sueeeeeeeey, chop sueeeeeeeeey!" I sing.

"London Bridge is a SWEET song! Wait, I know! You should take her to Paris and propose. That's where London Bridge is, right?" Jim asks, grabbing the bottle of tequila off of the coffee table and taking a swig.

"I don't know. Carmela went to Paris and was all depressed and shit. I don't want Claire to be depressed when I propose."

Jim stared at me blankly.

"Who the fuck is this Carmela person? Are you cheating on Claire? I will FUCK YOU UP!" Jim yells.

"Dude, simmer down. Carmela Soprano. Remember? Tony sent her to Paris with her friend Ro so she could 'find herself'. It really was a beautiful gesture on his part since he was banging the Russian chick with one leg," I state.

"Hey, fuck face. You know these people only live in your television, right? THEY. AREN'T. REAL," Jim argues.

"Take it back," I whisper menacingly. "Take it back right now."

"FUCK YOU, SAM I AM!" Drew screams at his phone, holding it up in front of his face.

"And anyway, I think they moved London Bridge. It's in Arizona or some shit like that now," I explain as I took the bottle back from him and rest it on my thigh.

"WHAT THE FUCK ARE YOU SAYING?" Jim yells right in my ear. "London Bridge is in Arizona? When the fuck did this happen? Does London know about this? The queen has got to be pissed."

"It was on 'Real Housewives' so you know it's true," I state.

"Orange County or Atlanta?" Jim asks.

"Orange County, what the fuck is wrong with you? Does anyone even *watch* Atlanta?" I argue.

"YOU AND YOUR STUPID RED AND WHITE STRIPED HAT! FUCKING CATS DON'T WEAR HATS!" Drew screams in frustration before throwing his phone against the wall.

What the hell are we even talking about? I feel like I'm going to puke. And why the fuck is Drew meowing in the kitchen? Do we have a cat? Oh fuck, did I forget to feed a cat? Claire's going to kill me if I murdered her cat.

The last thing I remember before passing out is Jim telling me in a moment of drunken brilliance that Claire would marry me if I fed her lobster and that we should call the queen and ask her if her she would trade us some Grey Poupon for the bridge she doesn't know she lost.

9. NO NUT SHOTS BEFORE LUNCH

The muffled vibrations of my cell phone from its spot under my pillow forces my eyes open. I blink the sleep out of them, pull my ear plugs out of each ear, and slide my hand under my pillow to answer the phone.

"Jesus, Claire. What the hell is that noise? It sounds like a monster. Is there a monster in your house?"

I chuckle at Jenny's question and roll over onto my back and look over at Carter who's fast asleep next to me.

"No, there isn't a monster in my house," I whisper. "That growling snort you hear is Carter snoring."

Once again I thank the good Lord for blessing me with the best earplugs in the world. Not something people typically give thanks for, but I am pretty sure God felt slighted because he is only remembered for the big stuff. I firmly believe there is a special place for me in heaven because I remember to thank him for Southern Butter Pecan coffee creamer and Coochy Cream shaving gel.

"Wow, he really needs to get that checked out," Jenny informs me. "You know, I read something the other day that maybe he should try. It said taking those relaxative things for a few days will make your whole body healthier. Maybe that would fix his sinuses."

"Did you say *relaxative*? Jenny, what the hell is a relaxative?"

I fling the covers off of me and sit up in bed so I can wake up a little more and be able to talk to her with a clear head. I doubt it will help, but here's to hoping.

"You know," she says with a huff, "R-E-L-A-X-A-T-I-V-E."

The fact that she feels the need to enunciate the word like *I* am the one with the problem and my inability to understand is irritating *her* makes me want to shank her.

82

"I heard the word. I just don't know what the hell you're talking about," I complain as I get out of bed and stretch before making my way out into the hall.

"You know, those pills you take to flush out your system. Relaxatives."

I open Gavin's bedroom door across the hall from our room and peek in on him. He was still out, lying on his back horizontally across his bed with his head hanging off of the edge. There's no way that can be comfortable but I'm not about to move him back up to his pillow and run the risk of waking him up before I've had my coffee. I shut the door quietly and go back to dealing with Jenny while I head to the kitchen.

"I think you mean *laxatives*," I tell her with a sigh. "And they aren't really supposed to be used to flush out your system. Where the hell did you even read that about snoring?"

"Google. So you know it's true. Tell Carter to try it and you can thank me with chocolate when it works," she replies.

I stop in my tracks in the kitchen doorway at the sight before me, unable to even formulate a reply to Jenny about how making Carter shit his brains out most likely would not stop his snoring.

"So anyway, I was calling to ask you if Drew was still at your house. I got a text from him last night as I was leaving your shop that the Cat in the Hat told him he should spend the night. I have no idea what that meant, but as long as I got the whole bed to myself I didn't care."

After the girls had helped me put together the huge chocolate and cookie order last night for a wedding today, we all left to go home. Gavin had fallen asleep in the car so when I got in the house, I bypassed the kitchen and went straight down the hall to his bedroom and then put myself to bed next to a snoring Carter.

I don't know whether I should be happy that I didn't see this sight last night or not. On his back, with his arms and legs flung out to the side, is Drew. Asleep. ON MY KITCHEN TABLE. His ass now

83

rests exactly where I usually put the salt and pepper shakers.

"Yes, he's still here. I need to hang up now so I can beat his ass," I tell her as I walk up to the table, hold the phone between my cheek and shoulder, and then use both of my hands to shove him as hard as I could. His limp body slides easily across the table and crashes to the floor on the other side.

"Don't hurt my pookie-bear!" Jenny yells through the phone.

I walk around the table and stand by Drew's head, looking down at him as he groans.

"Wow, did I sleep on your floor all night?" Drew asks as he opens his eyes and glances up at me from the floor. "You really should consider putting in carpet instead of hardwood. This stuff is really uncomfortable."

Drew rolls over onto all fours with another groan and slowly stands up, twisting and turning as he moves to try and crack his back.

"Get. Out. Of. My. House," I tell him as calmly as I can without screaming and waking up Carter and Gavin.

"Tell him I love him and that my vagina misses him!" Jenny yells excitedly.

"Jenny says to tell you that you need to GET YOUR SORRY ASS OUT OF MY HOUSE!"

"Heeeeey, that's not what I said," Jenny mutters.

"Jenny, I'll call you back."

I hang up the phone and open my mouth to tell Drew to get out of my house again, just in case he hadn't hear me the first two times, when Gavin comes running into the kitchen in his pajamas.

"Hi, Uncle Drew!" he says excitedly as he runs up to Drew. Just as Drew starts to bend over to greet him, Gavin pulls his elbow back and catapults his fist right between Drew's legs.

Drew falls down on his knees with a yelp and I laugh. I know you're not supposed to laugh when your child does something he shouldn't, but I feel this was deserved. I had just found Drew passed out in the middle of the table we eat on. He's lucky I didn't stop Gavin and give him a baseball bat first.

"Gavin, dude, we had a rule!"

At the sound of his voice, I turn to find Carter walking into the room rubbing sleep from one eye. He kisses my cheek as he steps around me and kneels down to Gavin's level.

"Gavin, what was our rule?" Carter asks while Drew clutches his junk, alternating between coughing and making some strange whining noise that reminds me of the sound a balloon makes when you pinch and stretch the opening of it and slowly let the air out.

"No nut shots before lunch," Gavin replies solemnly.

"Right, no nut shots before lunch. And do you know what time it is?" Carter asks.

"I can't tell time," Gavin states.

"Have you had lunch yet?" Carter asks.

"No."

"Then it's before lunch. Tell Uncle Drew you're sorry."

Gavin sighs and turns to face Drew who has finally stopped moaning and is in the process of getting back to his feet.

"I'm sorry I shot you in the nuts before lunch," Gavin mumbles. "Can I have some cereal now?" he asks as he looks at me and away from Drew.

"Sure, baby," I tell him with a smile as I take his hand and walk him toward one of the kitchen chairs. I take one look at the table and veer us in the direction of a bar stool at the island instead. I need to bleach Drew's ass from that table before we ever eat there again.

"My testicles are sitting in my stomach right now. How can you even think about cereal?" Drew asks as he limps over to the counter and grabs his keys.

"Your tentacles are dumb and I'm hungry," Gavin replies around a mouthful of Lucky Charms as I finish pouring the milk in his bowl.

"Whatever, kid. Thanks for letting me crash, guys. I'm gonna make like a fetus and head out."

I let out a big sigh when the door closes behind Drew.

"The next time I find him asleep on any piece of furniture in this house, I'm taking it out on you," I tell Carter.

He comes up behind me and wraps his arms around my waist and places a kiss to the curve of my neck.

"Deal," he replies as he rests his chin on my shoulder.

"You realize you made a rule with your son that states he has permission to punch people in the nuts *after* lunch, correct?"

"Yeah. It sounded good at the time when I made the rule. He had just shown me for the second time the power of his punch, and I was crippled on the ground at the park at the time, so I might not have had full brain function."

I stand there for a few minutes, enjoying the feel of Carter's arms around me as we watch our son scarf down his breakfast.

"I want to have your parents over for dinner," I told him as I turn in his arms and rest my hands against his chest. "I want to cook something really delicious, ply them with alcohol and chocolate, and make them like me. Or at least drunk enough to forget why they don't."

Carter chuckles and tightens his arms around me.

"Babe, they like you. I swear. My grandma even said you had spunk."

"That's old person speak for 'she's bat shit crazy and I'm afraid I'll bust a hip just being in the same room with her when I beat her ass.' I need a chance to make a better first impression," I explain.

"Your FIRST, first impression was just fine. You're forgetting who my best friend is. The first time they met Drew he crashed at our house one night in high school. My mom found him sleepwalking in the middle of the night. She walked into the living room and he was peeing on the couch. Believe me, they've seen it all," Carter reassures me.

"Drew is a moron. He shouldn't be allowed in public without a leash and a handler. I am the mother of their grandson. I shouldn't be talking about a whale's vagina on their Facebook pages. I should be posting pictures of their grandson at a museum studying the works of Michelangelo and posting status messages about my philanthropic work like holding babies in orphanages and hugging homeless people."

Carter stares at me quizzically for a few minutes.

"Will you say something?" I demand.

"Sorry, I'm just trying to figure out if you're serious or not."

"Why the hell wouldn't I be serious? I could totally be that person. I could be that person and you wouldn't even know it," I tell him indignantly as I cross my arms in front of me.

"Oh, I'm pretty sure I would notice if you suddenly turned into a completely different person," he tells me with a laugh.

"Are you saying I'm not a nice person? That I wouldn't cuddle a strange baby or make a homeless guy feel special? Because I would totally do all of that. Maybe I've already been doing it behind your back. Maybe instead of going to the dentist the other day I went to a PETA meeting and threw fake blood on rich people wearing fur. Maybe Gavin has been learning French at night while you're at work."

I crane my neck behind me to look at Gavin.

"Hey, say something in French," I tell him.

"I like french fries," he tells me as he looks up from his cereal bowl with milk dripping down his chin.

"See?" I say as I turn back to face Carter. "He can already use a word in a sentence."

"Okay, stop. Take a deep breath. Of course I think you're a nice person. I think you're an amazing person. But I think we all know that you are not a

Stepford Wife and Gavin isn't conjugating French verbs while listening to Mozart."

"MY WIENER EXPLODED!"

Carter drops his arms from my waist, and I jump around in horror at Gavin's scream.

"Never mind. I just spillded milk on it. I have a milk wiener now."

I shake my head and turn back to face Carter.

"I rest my case," he says with a laugh.

I frown and try to act indignant but Carter can see the wheels turning in my head and cuts me off.

"I love both of you exactly the way you are. I love that you have no filter, and I adore that Gavin can make grown men cry. There is not one thing I would change about either one of you, and if anyone doesn't like it, they can kiss my ass. You guys are my life and my family now. Nothing else matters."

Carter bends down and presses a soft kiss to my lips and pulls me tighter against him. His words push aside some of my fears about his family, but it doesn't change the fact that I still want to try again with them. I plan on spending a very long time with this man. I'm still not sold on the whole marriage thing, but I still want him in my life forever, which means I needed to find a way to get on his parents' good side one way or another. If I have to get them drunk, so be it.

"Thank you. But I still want to have your parents over for dinner. I want to at least show them I can act like an adult most of the time."

10. CEILING FAN BASEBALL

"Oh my God! You guys are doing it all wrong. Obviously we need to go over these rules one more time. The dinner roll needs to be thrown *under* hand at the ceiling fan. That's the only way you'll get the arc you need for a good pitch. We're not going for speed, people. We're going for accuracy. Someone pop another batch in the oven so we can start the third inning for fuck's sake!"

After my mother finishes her explanation, she hefts the wooden cutting board up to her shoulder by the handle and readies herself for the pitch.

"Carter, if you bend over like that in front of me again, I might have to grab that sweet little tush of yours and call your mother and thank her."

I'll toast to that.

I raise my wine glass in the air for a toast while Drew does a couple of practice throws.

"I got this one, Mom. Dear Mrs. Ellis, thank you for pushing Carter out of your vagina and having such good genes that he has the most perfect ass I've ever seen," I say with a snort and a wink in Carter's direction.

"Um, thank you?"

My eyes go wide and with my wine glass still held above my head. I turn around slowly and find Carter's parents standing in the dining room doorway looking around at the scene in front of them in shock and awe...but mostly shock.

In hindsight, I should have known better than to listen to anything my mother suggests. Carter's parents had canceled coming to dinner at the last minute because his father was feeling under the weather. How was I supposed to know they would just show up an hour after dinner was over only to find me talking about her vagina, her son naked from the waist up with his shirt tied around his forehead, my dad sitting in the far

89

corner of the room with a bowl of mashed potatoes in his lap, Drew wearing an apron that said, "I didn't wash my hands before I fondled your meat," and Liz and Jenny crawling on all fours around the kitchen table, eating the broken pieces of dinner rolls off of the floor and giggling.

From now on when my mom says, "Beating a dead horse around a bush during a blue moon won't fix anything," I'm going to plug my ears and walk away.

Two hours earlier

"Does it make me a bad person if I feel really bad that your dad doesn't feel well, but feel even worse for myself because I did all this work and now they won't see it?"

Carter laughs and uncorks a bottle of wine.

"I still can't believe you thought their anniversary was the perfect day to have my parents over for dinner."

He pours me a glass of wine as I slide on oven mitts and pull the roast out of the oven.

"Daddy, I wanna help cook the food. What can I make?" Gavin asks as he comes bounding into the kitchen.

"Well, I think Mommy's got everything just about done. How about you take people's coats as they come in the door?"

The doorbell rings and Gavin, happy with the chore he has just been given, scampers off to see who is here.

"I know. It was a crazy idea to do this on their thirtieth anniversary, but I just wanted them to come here, have a nice, family dinner and see that I can be a normal, well-balanced adult. What better day to do that than on a day where everyone has to rejoice in their love, and it would be against the spirit of the marriage in general if anyone said the words whore, vagina, or penis out loud?"

I set the roaster pan on top of the stove and toss the oven mitts onto the counter. The sound of Gavin answering the door puts a halt to our conversation.

"Hi, Uncle Jim. Give me a dollar and I'll cut you."

Carter hands me the glass of Chardonnay and sighs.

"How did he go from, 'Can I take your coats please?' to 'I'm going to murder you for ringing the doorbell.'?"

I shrug and take a sip of the chilled wine.

"Maybe it's a blessing in disguise your parents couldn't come. I think we need a trial run to get this normal thing down pat first," I tell him with a smile.

"I am *not* going to say I told you so," Carter says with a kiss to my cheek.

"Good. Because if you did, I'd have Gavin take your coat and shiv you."

Carter walks out of the room when the doorbell rings again to make sure Gavin doesn't make good on his cutting threats.

With my wine glass in one hand, I start placing serving spoons in all of the side dishes and then pull out the big carving knife so Carter can cut the roast. While I work, I listen to the sounds of a football game coming from the television in the living room and my family and friends talking quietly amongst themselves as they show up. Even if Carter's parents couldn't make it, I know it will still be a good day and a great dinner.

"Claire Bear! Who is this sexy beast you have answering the door for you now?"

I choke on a mouthful of wine and turn to see my mother walk into the room with her arm linked through Carter's. "Have you been working out, Carter?" she asks as she rubs her hand up and down his bicep.

"Mom? What are you doing here? I thought you were going to an art gallery opening?" I ask.

She lets go of Carter's arm and practically skips across the kitchen to me, wrapping me in her arms and squealing in delight.

91

"Nonsense! When you called the other night and said you were nervous about making a good impression on Carter's stuffy parents, I knew I needed to be here for my best girl," she explains as she pulls back and fiddles with a lock of my hair that has come loose from my pony tail.

"Oh my God, Mom! I never said his parents were stuffy!" I argue as I smacked her hand away from my hair. My mother, while well-meaning, treats me more like a best friend than a daughter and possesses even less of a filter between her brain and her mouth than I do.

I give Carter a look of embarrassment and beg him with my eyes to not listen to a word she said. My mother continues talking like I'm not even there.

"Now, Carter, you look positively yummy and not at all tired. Shouldn't you be exhausted from staying up all night sleeping with my daughter? Claire, why aren't you keeping this man up until the wee hours of the morning having lots of sex?"

"Jesus, Mom! Can you tone it down a bit please?" I beg.

Carter had met my mom the day we moved in when she came to help us unpack and has stopped by for dinner several times since then. He is quite familiar with the way she acts but that doesn't mean I can't try to nip it in the bud before it gets out of hand.

"What? Can't a mother be concerned for her daughter? I just want to make sure your vagina doesn't get full of cobwebs like before. Those things can take a pounding so don't worry about breaking anything. I once pulled a muscle in my vagina. Did I ever tell you that story?"

So much for the no vagina talk today.

I chug the rest of my glass of wine, reach for the bottle on the counter, fill the glass back up, and then took a swig right from the bottle before setting it back down.

"Mom, did I tell you dad brought Sue with him today? You know, the woman he's been seeing? She's really nice. And never, ever talks about pounding vaginas. Ever."

I think maybe making my mom a teensy bit jealous will deter her from all things inappropriate but sadly I'm mistaken. Sometimes I still forget just how cordial my parents divorce was.

"Ooooooh goody!" she squeals, clapping her hands together like a two-year-old. "I've wanted to meet her ever since your father first told me about her. We have so much to talk about. I wonder if he's used his Sean Connery accent on her yet and tried that move where he puts his foot on the headboard and then thrusts-"

"STOP! Jesus Christ, please stop," I plead before taking another big gulp of my wine. "Carter, can you let everyone know dinner is ready and we're doing it buffet style. They can all come in here and fill up their plates before sitting down at the table. If you need me, I'll be in here with my head in the oven."

~

An hour later everyone is still picking at their food after going back for seconds and thirds. My mom sits next to Sue and the two of them have been whispering and giggling like school girls through the entire meal, stopping every once in a while to glance over at my dad before falling into a fit of hysterics all over again.

"Hey, Claire, does this apple pie have nuts in it? I don't like nuts," Drew states.

"I like nuts. Nuts are delicious," Gavin pipes up, taking a big bite of apple pie to prove it.

"Well, *I* don't like nuts," Drew argues.

"Guys, that's enough nut talk," Liz complains as she pours herself another glass of wine from the bottle in the middle of the table.

"I'M GOING TO PUT MY NUTS ON ALL OF YOU!" Gavin yells through a mouthful of food.

Carter clamps his hand over Gavin's mouth and then leans over to quietly tell him it isn't polite to yell at the table.

"So, Claire's mom, do you have any good stories to tell us about your little cupcake when she was growing up? Any slumber parties with naked pillow fights or lesbian experimentation?" Drew asks.

"What's a lez bean? Is that like a lima bean? I don't like lima beans. I am NOT going to eat a lez bean," Gavin declares.

"Oh, you'll change your mind about that someday," Drew tells him with a wink.

"Gavin, how about you go pick out a movie, and I'll put it on in the living room?" Carter suggests. He obviously doesn't want our son learning about the fine art of carpet munching just yet.

Gavin lets his fork clamor to his plate, jumps down off of his chair, and takes off running to the DVD shelf in the living room.

"Sorry, Drew, my childhood was pretty uneventful," I tell him, bringing the conversation back to the original subject. "No one has anything even remotely interesting to tell," I inform him as I hold my glass across the table towards Liz so she can give me a refill.

My mom nods in agreement and gives Drew a sad look.

"Unfortunately she's right. Claire was a very boring child. She liked to read and take naps. We used to invent things to do just to mess with her and try to fuck her up a little bit. She was entirely too well-rounded. It was disturbing. George, remember that time you had your friend Tim call the house when she was eight because she wasn't listening to you? Didn't he pretend he was Santa Clause?"

My dad leans back in his chair and comes an inch away from sticking his hand in the waistband of his pants in post-dinner bliss before he realizes he isn't alone in his own home. He quickly switches directions and moves his arm to the back of Sue's chair.

"Yep, she was being a mouthy little shit so I had Tim call and put the fear of Santa into her," he says with a chuckle.

"Hey, that wasn't funny. He told me I was a very bad little girl and that he'd been watching me. He said he lived in the basement and came up at night to watch me sleep. He's the reason I still take the basement stairs two-at-a-time when I run up them and why I called America's Most Wanted when I was nine because there was some killer on the loose hiding in people's basements," I explain. "I told them the killer was Santa, that he called me the year before, and that he was probably still in our basement."

"I remember that afternoon. The police questioned us for two hours so they could make sure we weren't harboring a criminal," my mother states. "That was such a long, boring day."

"No, don't worry about me. I was totally fine," I deadpan.

"Oh quit your bitchin'. It wasn't that bad. You're still alive, aren't you?" my dad asks. "And don't lie, Rachel. They only questioned us for about thirty seconds. Then you asked them if they wanted a joint and all was forgotten. Cops were way more fun back then," he says to the rest of the table.

I turn towards Carter. "Never, ever ask me again why I am the way I am. NEVER. AGAIN," I whisper.

"I did walk in on her playing with her Barbie's one time, and she had them all undressed, humping each other. It was some weird sex circle, and Ken was sitting in the middle just watching them, fully dressed. I wanted to light some incense and set the mood for her, but then I saw she had one of the horses in the circle of sex and it just got disturbing at that point. I never knew Barbie was into bestiality," my mother states solemnly.

I lean forward and start banging my head softly on the table.

"Nice! Getting freaky with the Barbie dolls. I like it," Drew exclaims.

"I think in honor of this family dinner, we need to remember the best part about our holiday dinners,

Rachel," my dad tells her with a gleam in his eye. "Ceiling fan baseball."

My parents start laughing as they remember dinners of the past, and I just continue to bang my head harder.

This was supposed to be a nice, peaceful dinner.

"Oh my God! I remember ceiling fan baseball from high school!" Liz says excitedly. "Except didn't we play it with tater tots a few times?"

"Yes, we've been known to make substitutions," my mother states.

"Okay, what the hell is ceiling fan baseball? It's not what I think it is, right?" Drew asks as he looks back and forth between my parents. They each look at me expectantly. Liz is practically bouncing up and down in her chair in excitement.

Oh what the hell.

I roll my eyes and drain my glass of wine in one gulp, slamming it back to the table with a *thunk.*

"Alright, fine. Carter, grab the wooden cutting board with the handle. Liz, put all the extra rolls on the stove into a basket. Jim, turn the ceiling fan on low and Drew, move the table to the side."

Everyone stares at me with their mouths open for exactly three seconds, and then they all jump into action and start gathering supplies.

"I'll get more booze!" Jenny announces happily.

"I got the mashed potatoes," my dad states casually.

"What do we need mashed potatoes for?" Carter asks as he walks back into the room with the cutting board, a.k.a "baseball bat".

"Claire, this man is hot as balls but he's kind of dumb," my mother says as she pats Carter's cheek affectionately. "The mashed potatoes are the catcher's mitt. Duh."

11. MOMMY!

I think it's safe to say that my parents will never understand the whirlwind that is Claire and her family. I'm okay with that. It's not like I've ever been that close to them anyway. Their parenting style had always been a bit more standoffish than most. I think it's one of the main reasons I knew I needed to do right by Claire and Gavin. I never want my son to feel like there is anything even remotely more important to me than him. Don't get me wrong. My parents are good people. They love me and they have done a good job raising me. They had sent me to the best schools and had high hopes for my future. When I dropped out of college because it bored the shit out of me, they didn't take it very well. They had wanted me to be a doctor or a lawyer and share their country club membership. They like things calm, neat, orderly, and pretentious. They most definitely aren't ceiling fan baseball-playing people, and they never will be. It had taken them a while to stop trying to fit me into a certain mold and realize they need to just let me make my own choices and live my own life. They had been really excited to find out they were grandparents and I know they will be good at it. On the bright side, at least Gavin will have someone in his life who could teach him how to sit on the board of a company, complain about paying taxes, and hide money from the government. Since he already has people showing him how to swear like a truck driver and throw food at ceiling fans during dinner, I do believe this will make him the most well-rounded human being on the planet.

It takes a lot of explaining and even more wine to get Claire on board with my line of thinking. She wants everyone to like her and considers herself a failure because my parents have only seen her at her worst. When I tell her that after twenty-five years *I* have yet to impress my parents and therefore she shouldn't let it get to her, she finally relents and decides against writing an apology note to them in chocolate on their front yard.

After my mother apologizes for showing up unexpectedly, and Drew throws a wild pitch into the fan that results in a dinner roll right to her neck, my parents realize the importance of calling ahead. They do their best to not make faces as they tiptoe around clumps of bread that litter the dining room floor to find an available seat. My father explains he thought he was coming down with a cold but after a short nap, he felt much better so they decided to stop by for dessert. Claire does her best to stick to the original plan of plying them with a bunch of alcohol and sweets to suck up to them, but after thirty minutes of Rachel trying to get my mother to admit she would love to try a threesome some day and goading my father to confess he dropped acid in the sixties, my parents decide it's past their bedtime.

After they leave, everyone helps clean up before they head to their own homes. When the last dish is put away and the final crumb is swept from the floor, we finally have the house all to ourselves and nothing can be heard except the ticking of the clock in the living room.

I walk into the kitchen after putting Gavin to bed to find Claire standing in front of the sink, staring out the window, lost in thought. I don't want her to feel guilty about my parents. I won't let them make her feel like anything less than the amazing woman I know her to be.

I come up behind her and slide my hands around her waist and clasp them together on top of her stomach. I rest my chin on her shoulder, waiting for her to speak.

"So. This was a fun day," she says sarcastically, bringing her hands up to rest on top of mine.

I turn my face and place a kiss on the side of her neck, inhaling the subtle hint of chocolate that always lingers on her skin.

"Actually, it was a very fun day. I had no idea you ever called America's Most Wanted," I tell her with a smile. "And that Barbie likes horse cock. Who knew?"

Her body shakes with laughter.

"Hey, don't judge me. Ken had underwear that wouldn't come off. What's a girl to do in that situation?" she asks as she turns into my embrace, slides her arms around me, and rests her cheek against my chest. "I was an only child with two crazy parents. Unless I wanted to hang out in the basement with my mother and smoke pot, there wasn't much else to do other than have Barbie orgies."

I laugh along with her and rub my hands in slow circles around her back.

"You can still run you know. If you want to make like the Road Runner and bust through the door leaving an imprint of your body behind, I won't blame you."

She looks up at me and smiles but I can tell she is kind of serious.

"Listen to me. Nothing matters but you, me, and Gavin. There is absolutely nothing that either one of our families can do to ruin this."

Ask her to marry you. Do it now!

"Claire…"

"Don't say it," she warns.

What the fuck? Can she read my mind? Claire, nod once if you can hear me.

"Don't tell me it was no big deal and that you don't care what your parent's think."

Oh thank God.

"Fine, I won't say it. I'll just think it."

Will you marry me? Will you marry me? Why the fuck is this so hard to say? There is nothing else more important right now than asking this question!

"I have a great idea. How about you take my mind off of everything by having sex with me on the kitchen counter," she says with a wag of her eyebrows.

Okay, this might trump the proposal.

Before I can stop her…oh who am I kidding? Like I'd really stop her from banging me in the kitchen. She leans up on her tiptoes and presses her mouth to

99

mine. The kiss quickly turns deeper and her tongue sweeping through my mouth instantly makes me hard. I pull away from her mouth long enough to lift her up onto the counter next to the sink. Her legs wrap around my waist and her hands go to work unbuttoning my jeans. Before I can even take another breath, her hand is inside my boxers, wrapping around my length.

"Fuck," I mutter, leaning my forehead against hers as she works her small hand from base to tip, tortuously slow. As my hips rock with the movements of her hand, I slide my palms up the outside of her bare thighs, my fingers inching slowly under the hem of her skirt until I wrap them around the strings of her thong that rest on her hips.

She unwinds her legs from around my waist and lets them dangle off of the edge of the counter so I can slide the black, lacy scrap of material off of her and fling it to the floor.

My eyes travel up her long, smooth legs, and her skirt pushes up to the top of her thighs. I let my hands follow the movement of my eyes, touching every inch of skin I look at. I part her thighs as I go, sliding my hands around her hips to cup her ass and bring her body closer to the edge of the counter.

Her hands move to the waistband of my boxer briefs and I almost whimper at the loss of her warm palm and fingers stroking me into oblivion. She uses both hands to push my boxer briefs down my hips just far enough for my cock to free itself.

I step closer between her thighs until the head of my erection meets her wet center. Gritting my teeth with the need to bury myself inside of her, I slide the tip of my cock up through her heat and circle it around her clit. Her legs slide back up the outside of my thighs, and she locks her feet behind my back, her ankles digging into my ass as she pulls me harder against her, and I slip inside of her one slow inch at a time.

"Jeeeeeesus, you feel good," I whisper against her lips as I rock my hips against her.

"This is the best *phone call* we've ever made," she says with a laugh as she wraps her arms around my shoulders.

"I've never made a *phone call* in the kitchen before. It always seemed unsanitary," I state as Claire lifts her hips to meet my thrusts.

"Please don't make me think about the fact that you just sliced a roast on this counter," she says between moans.

"At least we're doing this *after* I cut the meat. Otherwise we would have served our family and friends ass-roast with a side of sex juices."

Claire's fingers slide through the back of my hair and clutches onto it so hard I wince and slow down my movements.

"Seriously? Do you want me to throw up on you while we're doing this? Never, ever use that sentence again."

I chuckle and pull her body tighter against mine, wrapping my arms around her. I try to keep my movements slow but it just feels too fucking good. I kiss a trail down her neck and start to swivel my hips in a circle. Claire's fingernails dig into my shoulder blades, and I feel her entire body shudder.

"Oh my God, keep doing that," she moans.

I should ask her to marry me now. If I do it while she's coming, she probably won't be able to say no. It would be physically impossible. Like performing a sex exorcist. THE POWER OF THE ORGASM COMPELS YOU!

"Oh fuck!" she cries as she pushes herself harder against me and lets her head fall back against the cabinet behind her as her orgasm builds.

Marry me, marry me, marry me.

"Yes! Oh my God yes!"

I wonder if I could pretend that conversation just happened outside *of my head and convince her of it. Just start going around telling people she said yes. "Yes, Grandma, we're getting married! What's that you say? How did I do it? Oh, I was fucking her on the kitchen counter, you know, where we prepare food, and it just slipped out! No, not my penis. The question."*

I smack a hand down on the counter next to her to hold myself steady as I plunge in and out of her faster and harder, trying to banish all thoughts of talking to my grandmother about slippery penises.

It helps that every time with Claire is like the first time. Just without all the booze, virginity robbing, and not knowing each other's names. I know more than ever that this is the person I want to spend the rest of my life with. I slide my other hand off of her ass and glide my fingers down to where we are connected. Claire lets out a gasp as I touched her with the tips of my fingers and draw her orgasm out of her. She comes quickly and moans my name, her breath hot against my ear. It's the sexiest thing in the world and my own release shoots its way up through my body and explodes out of me. I bury my face into the side of her neck and shout the words I've been worrying about for weeks. Well, I don't shout them so much as muffle them really loudly since my mouth is pushed against her skin.

We clutch onto each other for several minutes, breathing heavy and not uttering a word.

Shit! She's probably mortified I asked her to marry me while I came and thinks it's just post orgasmic bliss or something equally as fucked up. That's why she isn't saying anything.

I pull my head out of the crook of her neck and chance a look at her. She's looking at me funny, almost like she felt a little sick to her stomach just from the sight of me.

Oh that's just super. The thought of marrying me makes her want to hurl.

"Um, Carter?"

"It's okay. You don't have to say anything," I tell her quickly.

I think it's safe to say my humiliation level at this moment is at an all time high. My penis is still inside of her. Does she WANT to make it shrivel up and die by discussing this?

102

"No, I really think we need to talk about this," she pleads with a worried look on her face.

I laugh uncomfortably. "Nope, no we don't. Let's just pretend it never happened. I've already forgotten."

She pushes on my shoulders and holds me at arm's length.

"Carter!" she scolds.

"I'm sorry, were you saying something?"

She huffs and rolled her eyes, clearly irritated with me that I don't want to have a nice, friendly conversation about how she'd rather yak up a fur ball than become my wife.

"Cut it out! This is serious."

As a heart attack. Or a penis dying in a vagina from a broken heart.

"I'm pretty sure we need to talk about the fact that you screamed 'MOMMY!' when you came," she hisses angrily.

"Whoa that's kinky, Carter! Who knew you had it in ya?"

Claire yelps in surprise and my head jerks around at the sound of Rachel's voice in our kitchen.

"MOM!" Claire yells as she tightens her thighs around me in an effort to get us closer and shield the fact that we are still intimately connected.

"Tsk, tsk. Shouldn't Carter be the one shouting that?" Rachel asks with a laugh. "Sorry to interrupt kitchen sex. Great idea by the way. Did I ever tell you about the time I had sex in the kitchen of a McDonald's?"

Claire growls and narrows her eyes at her mother.

"Another time maybe! Just stopped back to get my purse that I left here," she says as she takes a few steps over to the kitchen table and picks it up off of one of the chairs. "You kids have a nice night. And may I just say you have a very nice ass, Carter. Claire, don't forget to do your kegels."

With that, she turns and breezes out of the kitchen, and we hear the front door open and close.

"What was that you said earlier about neither one of our families being able to ruin anything?" Claire asks sarcastically.

12. STINKY WIENER TICKS AND TWICE BAKED POTATOES

"Dude, she thought you called out 'Mommy'? Oh sweet Jesus, that is the best thing I've ever heard! Seriously. You just made my week." Drew laughs as he pats my back.

"It's always a pleasure when my humiliation amuses you."

Drew continues laughing and shaking his head as he works on the car panel in front of him. We have three minutes to do our job on the car in progress before the conveyor belt starts moving the car down the line again for the next pair of workers.

"How in the hell did you diffuse the situation? That's what I want to know!" Jim walks up behind me to grab a clipboard off of the table and makes some notes, waiting patiently for my answer.

"Well, having her mother walk in on us helped. Claire was completely focused on her making comments about my ass rather than on the fact that I may or may not have called out something completely inappropriate during sex. Is it wrong that I'd rather she thought I *did* call her 'Mommy' instead of just admitting I really said 'marry me'?" I ask.

"I dated a girl once who liked to call me 'Daddy' in the sack. It was kind of hot until I actually met her dad. He looked like Danny Devito, but shorter and with less hair. He always smelled like farts and swiss cheese and liked to bark at hot chicks when they'd walk by him in public," Drew tells us.

"I take that back. It would have been less painful for her to think I proposed than to hear that story," I say disgustedly.

"So what's the plan now? So far a baseball game and post-coital hasn't worked for ya. Got any other tricks up your sleeve?" Jim jokes.

"I was thinking about doing it over dinner maybe. Someplace really romantic. Isn't that what you said I should do that night after we tried on tuxes?"

105

Jim looks at me in confusion. "I did? I don't recall. Although I woke up at three in the morning in your bathtub with no pants on that night, so it's possible I had some really good ideas."

"Ooooooh! You should totally propose at our rehearsal dinner next weekend," Jim says excitedly as he slams the clipboard down on the table.

"Really? I don't know. It seems like kind of an intrusion on you and Liz. That's your special day."

"Slow down there, Miss Manners. I'm not asking you to have a double-wedding with us. Just pop the question over dinner. Please, God, give me something else to think about right now other than aisle runners, boutonnières, and swatches," Jim complains.

"Are you wearing a *Swatch Watch* for your wedding?" Drew asks, forming the letter "X" with his arms in front of him and pronouncing the words with flair.

"Funny. Just wait until Jenny gets her hooks in you and you have to deal with her psycho mother. Every time Mary Gates walks in the room and shows me a ribbon sample I want to say, 'Did you see that? The fuck I give. It went that way.' I'm about one tablecloth color away from just telling everyone to bring a side dish and a lawn chair to our backyard and have Drew get ordained on the internet to do the ceremony," Jim complains. "Liz asked me the other day what I thought about twice baked potatoes. How the fuck should I know? Was I supposed to be thinking about twice baked potatoes all this time? Is this where I went wrong? Are grown men *supposed* to have an opinion about twice baked potatoes?"

Jim looks like his head is about ready to explode. He stands there with his arms outstretched like he's pleading for understanding or some sort of man hug. Since Drew and I aren't the man-hugging type, Jim finally drops his arms and continues with his rant.

"And my parents, being the good Christian people they are, think one bottle of wine on every table is enough liquor. My mother's exact words were, 'If

106

we run out, we run out. People will just have to make do with water.'"

Drew's mouth drops open as the car we finished moves down the line and a new one follows in its wake.

"Water? At a wedding? I don't understand," he asks in confusion. "Did you invite Jesus? That's the only way that will be acceptable."

"Please, for the love of God, propose to Claire at the rehearsal dinner so my future mother-in-law will squeal in someone else's ear for one night. I beg of you," Jim pleads.

I think about Jim's suggestion while I get to work on the next vehicle. The restaurant where the rehearsal dinner will be held *is* a really beautiful place. And our friends will all be there to witness the event, something I'm sure Claire will love. The more I go over the idea in my head, the more excited I become. The rest of the night at work flies by as Drew and Jim help me come up with the perfect plan to ask Claire to be my wife.

~

The following Friday evening, Claire, Gavin, and I pull into the parking lot of Pier W, a beautiful landmark restaurant in Cleveland that is designed to resemble the hull of a luxury liner. Its location, perched high on a cliff overlooking Lake Erie, gives it a breathtaking view and makes me one hundred percent certain I have chosen the best location for a marriage proposal.

After a short run-through of the ceremony at the church where the wedding will be held the following afternoon, everyone is looking forward to a relaxing evening with good food and drinks. Jim and Drew keep eying me with furtive glances the entire time we are at the church, winking at me and nudging my arm whenever they can. I come close to punching Drew in the stomach directly under a statue of Mary at one point.

"Hey, Carter, can I pop you a question?"

107

It's the fourth time Drew has made a reference to asking a question, and I've had enough. The groomsmen are standing in a straight line at the side of the altar while the priest speaks quietly to Liz and Jim in the center of the aisle.

"Will you shut the fuck up already? Claire's going to get suspicious you dick-fuck!" I whisper angrily at him.

"Whoa, dude, slow your roll. You just said f-u-c-k in front of the Virgin Mary. Show some respect," Drew scolds.

"What's a virgin?" Gavin asks from his position standing next to me as he swings the ring bearer pillow around his head like a lasso.

"Uh, it's a kind of chicken," I stammer. "Very rare. No one talks about it."

It's impossible not to be nervous as I take Claire's hand and help her out of the car. My palms are sweating, and I hope she doesn't notice as I stand there for a minute staring at her while she helps Gavin out of his car seat.

She's so fucking beautiful I want to cry like a baby.

She closes Gavin's car door and catches me staring at her.

"Are you okay? You seem a little out of it," she says as she looked me over.

Shit, is my forehead sweating? Is she looking at me right now wondering why I look like a chubby man with a heart condition who just ate his weight in chicken wings and Jell-O salad at a buffet? That's not a good look to have when you want the woman you love to look into your eyes and pledge her undying love by saying 'yes' to marrying you.

"Mom, my stinky wiener ticks," Gavin states, interrupting the sweat fest and giving me time to wipe my forehead.

"Um, what does that mean?" Claire asks him.

"It means GET A MOVE ON! I wanna eat some beef turkey!"

The three of us turn and make our way up the sidewalk to the set of stairs that will lead us to the rock face where the restaurant sits.

Once inside the doors, the maître d' escorts us across the room to a long table set up in front of panoramic windows that overlook the lake. We are the last to arrive, as per the plan devised by Drew and Jim. The last three empty seats are strategically placed at the end of the table, the perfect spot for everyone to see what is going to happen.

Our friends are all in the midst of quiet conversations amongst themselves when we walk up but stop long enough to greet us and for Jim to make sure we know not to order any drinks since they are getting champagne. The mention of champagne is over exaggerated with a wink when Claire turns to help Gavin into his seat.

As the conversation moves to talk of the wedding the following day, I try to listen while going over my lines in my head. It doesn't seem appropriate to use the same speech I had prepared for the Indian's game proposal since there were words like "grand slam" and "switch hitter".

Hey, I never had said it was the best speech.

Since that plan had tanked, I needed to start from scratch. On our lunch hours at work every night this week, Drew and Jim helped me write the perfect words to say to Claire. Okay, *Jim* helped me write the perfect words. Drew wanted me to just throw a ping pong ball at her face, reminiscent of her bartending days at Fosters' Bar and Grill where she made up the game P.O.R.N. According to him, I should whip it at her chin and say, "That won't be the only ball bouncing off your chin if you say yes!"

After three rough drafts of the proposal and several uses of thesaurus.com, Jim and I had written the most perfect proposal ever. This night needs to be flawless. Claire will spend countless hours retelling the story of how I proposed to everyone she knows, and even a few strangers, for the rest of her life. She deserves the most romantic story to tell.

The waitress comes around a few minutes later to take everyone's order.

"So, little man, what can I get you?" she asks as she bends down to Gavin's level.

"I want a virgin," he states.

Claire starts choking on her water and Liz reaches over to pat her on the back.

"I'm sorry, what do want to order?" the waitress asks him in confusion.

"A virgin. I want to order a virgin," he repeats, looking at her like she was a moron.

"Don't we all, son. Don't we all," Jim's father mumbles from a few spots down, receiving a smack on the arm from his wife.

"I think he means chicken," I clarify sheepishly.

"Yes, because *that* makes perfect sense," Claire says under her breath as she picks up her water glass and attempts to take another sip.

With our orders taken, the waitress disappears and conversation resumes.

"Jim, I've been meaning to ask if you were able to finish hot gluing those crystals to all the ribbons for the church programs," Mrs. Gates asks. "And also, don't forget to put Preparation H under your eyes tomorrow morning."

Drew starts laughing and Jenny kicks him under the table.

"I'm totally calling him Hemorrhoid Head all day tomorrow." Drew leans over and whispers to me. "I know he's been stressed about the wedding, but I didn't realize it would cause ass itching under his eyes."

Jim's mom hears Drew and gives him a stern look that instantly wipes the smile off of his face.

"Andrew, it is well documented that this type of cream can reduce puffiness under one's eyes. Very effective when one needs to have their pictures taken," she states primly.

"Also very *funny* when one's eyes now have anal leakage," Drew says under his breath.

"Jim, before you leave tonight remind me to give you the magazine photos of the two different floral

110

arches for you to look at. You'll just need to tell the florist which one you want her to use at the reception tomorrow when she delivers the boutonnières," Liz's mom adds.

Jim is right. This woman is a walking, talking wedding robot.

"Jesus Christ, do it already before she starts talking about wedding favors and I grow a vagina," Jim begs in a low whisper.

I give him a nod to let him know I'm ready. A big grin breaks across his face as he completely ignores Weddingbot 2000 and signals our waitress while Claire is busy discussing the difference between good words and bad words with Gavin.

Jim and I had met with the manager of the restaurant and our waitress the day before to go over the plan for the evening. The waitress will bring over a tray of champagne for everyone at the table as soon as she is given the signal. At the bottom of Claire's glass will be the engagement ring I had dropped off this afternoon when I ran out to pick up Gavin's and my tux.

I couldn't believe it was finally time to do this. I am going to propose to the woman of my dreams who I thought I'd never see again after our one night in college.

The waitress is back and has served almost half the table their glasses of champagne. I figure it's now or never.

I reach down and clasp Claire's hand that rests on my thigh, bringing it up to my lips, trying to calm the frantic beating of my heart.

When she feels my lips on her hand, she turns to look at me.

"I love you so much, Claire," I say softly as I see the waitress move closer and closer to us out of the corner of my eye.

"I love you too, Carter," she replies with a smile.

The waitress only has two more people to serve before she gets to us. I know I need to speed things up a bit if I want to time everything just right.

"Oh my gosh, wait until you hear what Jenny said to me earlier. I can't believe I forgot to tell you," Claire says as she leans in closer to me and glances over my shoulder to make sure Jenny isn't listening.

I look behind me as well and see the waitress rounding the table, heading right for us. I need to be down on my knee when she places Claire's glass in front of her.

Shit!

"Claire, hold that thought. I have something I need to say."

She completely ignores me and turns sideways in her chair so she can face me and get closer.

"Wait, this is really good! You're going to love this," she says excitedly as my foot starts bouncing frantically on the floor when I see the waitress stop right behind Claire to say something to Gavin. "Okay, so Jenny said Drew's been acting funny lately. Talking about weddings and marriage proposals and asking her hypothetical questions like, 'If I were to propose to you, what would you want me to say?' Drew is so damn obvious."

I look back at Claire, barely registering what she is saying and wondering if it's bad manners to tell her to shut the hell up right before I ask her to marry me.

"Huh? What did you say?" I ask her as she continues to talk and I miss the last few sentences.

"I said Jenny thinks Drew is going to propose to her tonight. Can you believe that shit?"

My head slowly turns to face her, my mouth falling open in shock, the waitress with the champagne long forgotten.

"Drew? Propose? Tonight?"

Fuckshitballldamn!

"I know, right? First of all, they haven't been together that long and second – who the hell proposes at someone else's rehearsal dinner? That's in poor taste if you ask me. You're taking the spotlight off of the

112

soon-to-be-married couple and putting it on you. It's like a slap in the face to them. Like, 'Oh hey, look at me! I'm an asshole and want all eyes on me instead of the two people they should be on! Ha ha, I'm such an asshole, who has a camera to document my assholeness for all of eternity?'" Claire says with a laugh and a shake of her head for the imaginary asshole in her mind.

Except *I'm* the asshole! I'm the mother fucking asshole!

An arm slides between our bodies and in the haze of my asshole pity party, I realize there is a champagne glass attached to the end of it. I literally feel my brain shutting down. I hear a computerized voice in there counting backwards from five and feel like I'm in the movie *"The Hurt Locker"* and don't know whether to cut the red or the blue wire.

The red or the blue?? THE RED OR THE MOTHER FUCKING BLUE?!

Claire reaches for her glass of champagne.

You know how people always talk about how during a moment of panic they feel like they're in a dream and everything is in slow motion? I have never experienced that before and always just assume they are full of shit and trying to make their story sound better.

Well, I'm right.

This shit isn't moving in slow motion; it's moving faster than the speed of light, and I'm cutting the wrong wire and exploding into a complete jackass spaz.

My arm, as if completely detached from my body, flies away from its spot resting on the table, knocking over a lit candle, the salt shaker, my own glass of champagne, and two full water glasses until my hand grasps onto Claire's champagne flute right before it touches her lips.

I yank the glass out of her hand, sloshing expensive champagne everywhere in the process. In the back of my mind I could hear someone yelling, "Nooooooooooo!" and am completely oblivious to the fact that the bat shit crazy screamer in the middle of Pier W is me.

Not even taking one second to think about my actions or the fact that everyone in the place is looking at me in horror, I quickly bring the glass to my lips, tip my head back, and dump everything into my mouth, including the ring.

Drew leans over and whispers in my ear when I slam the empty glass back down on the table. "Dude, are you changing the plan? Because if the new plan is that you're going to try and shit out that ring, I gotta tell ya, that's not very romantic."

13. TEE TIME

I'm going to cry.

I'm going to cry like a God dammed baby and there's nothing I can do to stop it. It's getting hard to swallow because my throat is so tight, and I'm starting to feel like I'm at a rave with a really bad strobe light because of the way I keep blinking my eyes to keep the tears at bay.

Son of a bitch, I'm going to *ugly cry*. Some women can pull off crying without their make-up running or fluids leaking from every hole in their face but not me. I'm in a gorgeous gown, my hair is professionally done, my make-up is flawless and in three seconds I'm going to ruin it all by losing complete control of the muscles in my face. I'm going to try really hard to stay quiet which is going to fuck me over because it's going to force me to make sounds that you only hear in the middle of the night on the Discovery Channel. By the time I'm finished, I'm going to look like I have pink eye after being punched in the face by Mike Tyson.

This is all Liz's fault. Why does she have to look so beautiful?

We're standing in the alcove at the back of the church, just seconds away from walking down the aisle. The other bridesmaids have already left to meet their groomsmen at the front of the alter, the doors leading into the church closing behind them to keep the guests' first view of the bride a secret until the last minute.

Mrs. Gates is busy fluttering around Liz making last minute adjustments to the train of her dress and reminding her to smile, but not too much or the creases at the corners of her eyes will show in the pictures. She's standing up and squatting down over and over as she circles Liz, and I giggle-snort around the tears forming in my eyes since she reminds me of a horse on a merry-go-round. I suddenly want to ask Liz if she has a riding crop I can borrow so I can whip her mother and make her go faster.

"I can't believe you're getting married," I whisper to my best friend as we both ignore her mother reminding Liz to clench her butt cheeks as she walks.

"Me either," she says with a smile through her own tears.

"I love Jim and I know you two will be so happy together," I reassure her. "But as your best friend, it is my duty to tell you that should you need it, my car is right outside, fully gassed with the keys in the ignition and a suitcase with vodka in it in the trunk. I've also been keeping my pimp hand strong, just in case Jim gets out of line and needs a little bitch slap."

She laughs and I lean in to give her a quick hug, careful to avoid tugging on her veil or messing up any part of her. I do not need the wrath of Mary Gates raining down upon me.

"Thanks, BFF. I love you."

The sound of gagging and thumping interrupts our Hallmark card moment and we turned to see Jim's little cousin Melissa in her flower girl dress straddling Gavin on the floor and trying to choke him. Gavin flails and kicks beneath her, trying to dislodge her hands from around his neck.

"Hey!" I whisper-yell. They both cease all movement and turn to stare at me. "What are you doing?!"

Gavin shoves with all of his might and Melissa tumbles off of him. He scrambles up, grabbing his fallen ring bearer pillow and clutching it to his chest.

"She freaking hell took my pillow! Stupid punk!" Gavin says loudly.

"He kicked me in my no-no-zone!" Melissa complains with a stomp of her foot.

"Oh my," Mrs. Gates mutters.

"You should eat dirt!" Gavin turns and yells at Melissa.

"I will NOT eat dirt!" she counterattacks.

"EAT IT WITH YOUR CHICKEN FACE!"

It's complete and utter child anarchy and before I can pick a kid to yell at, the organ music changes and begins playing the song that I needed to walk down the aisle to with Gavin and Melissa right behind me.

I quickly bend down in front of both of them and stare them square in the face with as stern of an expression as I can muster.

"Both of you little monsters, listen up. As soon as you step foot out of those doors, you better have smiles on your faces and your outside voices duct taped inside your bodies. If you speak, push, shove, swear, argue, or even blink at each other I will haul your asses out of that church and lock you in the basement with the scary clowns."

I huff to emphasize my point and stand, tugging up the front of my strapless dress.

"If I see a clown, I'm going to punch him in the nuts."

"Gavin Allen!" I scold.

"What? We didn't step fru dose doors yet," he argues, pointing behind me.

"Kid has a point," Liz whispers.

"Behave," I whisper through clenched teeth as I turn and nodded to the two church attendants so they can open the double doors for my entrance.

"My mom's not afraid to punch a kid," I hear Gavin whisper to Melissa as I take my first step down the aisle.

Thankfully, my threat pays off and both kids make it to the front of the church without killing each other. The ceremony is beautiful and the only interruption came during communion.

Liz is Catholic so she had wanted a full, Roman Catholic service. Carter is a "sort-of" Catholic in that he was baptized, made his First Communion and everything else he was required to do while growing up, but he only goes to church for holidays, weddings, and funerals. Regardless, when it comes time for communion, he gets in line and takes Gavin with him since Gavin is on his side of the church through the ceremony.

I really don't believe in any one religion, but I have been known to sit in on a few services every once in a while just in case someone up there is taking notes. I sit in my seat in the front row with one other bridesmaid who isn't Catholic and we watch the procession and smile at those who walk by. I crane my neck and watch happily as Carter holds Gavin's hand while he stands in front of the priest and receives his little Jesus wafer. In the quiet serenity of the process, with only the beautiful sounds of the organ to fill the silence, Gavin's voice bursts through the tranquility.

"Whatchu got in your mouth?"

I bite my lip and cringe at how easily Gavin's voice carries through the church. Carter bends over and whispers something to Gavin as they turn and start to walk back to their seats in the front row on the opposite side of the church from me.

"GIMMEE WHATCHU GOT IN YOUR MOUTH!"

I cover my eyes with my hand but not before seeing Gavin try to shove his little hand into Carter's mouth. Carter smacks his hand away and as they both sit down, Carter pulls his cell phone out of the pants pocket of his tux and hands it over to Gavin. His face lights up with glee as he snatches the phone out of Carter's hand and sits down quietly next to him. Obviously, Carter is quickly learning that as a parent, nothing works quite as well as bribery. Seconds later the opening notes from Angry Birds blare through the soft din of organ music, and Carter quickly grabs the phone from Gavin to silence the sounds while Gavin yells, "Heeeey! I was playing that!"

The ceremony finally ends and we spend the next couple of hours getting pictures taken. Before I know it, we are finishing up dinner at the reception and the wait staff begin clearing tables. As part of the wedding party, we are all seated at the long head-table at the front of the room. It's always fun to sit facing a group of two hundred strangers so they can watch you eat.

Carter takes his seat next to me after a quick trip to the bathroom, and I noticed he was rubbing his shoulder in pain.

"What happened?"

"I passed Jenny and Drew on the way back from the bathroom. She wanted to know if I loved the *Balsa McChicken* we had for dinner," Carter explains with a raise of one eyebrow.

"I take it you told her it's called *balsamic chicken*?"

"No. I asked her if that was something new McDonald's was serving on their menu with the McRib. Drew punched me."

I glance around the room until I find my father and see him getting up from his table. He offers to head out early and take Gavin home with him as soon as he gets tired. I look at the chair next to me where Gavin is currently asleep on his stomach with his head, arms, and legs dangling down towards the floor.

"No, I didn't club him like a baby seal," I assure my dad as he puts his hands on the table and leans over it to get a look at his grandson.

"Your mother is starting to tell people about Tee Time. I think that's my cue to leave," my dad tells me as I stand with Carter while he scoops Gavin up into his arms and passes him off to my dad.

"What's Tee Time?" Carter asks as we watch Gavin sigh and snuggle his face into my dad's shoulder, muttering something about flashlights and donkey kicks.

My dad smiles evilly at Carter and then looks at me. "I'll leave you two to discuss the Rachel Morgan Tee Time tradition."

We say our good-byes and as the reception hall door closes behind them, my mother's voice comes over the microphone's speaker.

"TEE TIME! IT'S TEE TIME! Everyone meet over by the bar in five minutes!"

I close my eyes and sigh as I hear Jim let out an excited yell and jump up from his seat.

When I open my eyes, Carter is watching as a crowd of about twenty people, led by Jim, walk over to the bar.

"What is going on?"

"Carter! Now that you are part of this family, it's time you learned about the grand old tradition that is Tee Time," my mother exclaims as she pushes her way between us and grabs both of our arms to leads us to the bar. "This is an age old ritual that my family performs at every wedding to ensure the married couple lives a long, happy life together and that all of their ups and downs are in the bedroom."

Jim stands by the bar, bouncing on the balls of his feet in excitement as we made our way up to him.

"Mrs. Morgan! What's our first order of business at this Tee Time gathering?" he asks with a big grin.

"I do believe whiskey is the first on the agenda tonight, my handsome groom," she replies with a smack to his ass as she waves someone over from another table.

"Hold on, wait just a second!" Liz's mom yells as she comes running up to us. "The cake needs to be cut, and you still haven't done the first dance and the photographer still needs-"

My mom steps in front of Mary's path and puts her hand up to stop her from getting any closer to Jim.

"Mary, dear, you look stressed. When was the last time you used the bullet I gave you for your birthday last year and gave yourself a nice, big orgasm?"

My mother, after having dealt with Mary Gates for enough years, knows exactly how to divert her attention onto something else. It's nice to see her focusing on someone else's sex life for once. With Mary sputtering and at a loss for words, the wedding reception checklist is forgotten.

"I have to say, I'm a little bit astounded by the fact that you were still a virgin the night we met. How is it possible your mother never bought you a male hooker for your birthday?" Carter asks.

Jim lets out a cheer when he sees his mother-in-law practically running away from the bar and yells to the bartender for twenty shots of whiskey to go around.

"So really, Tee Time is just another excuse to get trashed at a wedding?" Carter asked.

"That would be correct," I reply as I take the shot glass filled with amber liquid that is handed to me. "Calling it Stupid Time would just be too obvious."

"I guess since you're drinking that means this gorgeous stud hasn't impregnated you again," my mother states as she takes her own.

"MOM!" I scold.

"What? Can you blame me for wanting another grandchild? You two make beautiful babies. The man obviously has super sperm. And by the looks of your late-night kitchen trysts, he still knows where to put it."

Mortification, party of one, your table is now ready.

"Did I ever tell you about the boyfriend I had in college who thought blow jobs could cause pregnancy? It's a shame really. I can suck a tennis ball through a crazy straw but he missed out."

Shouldn't there be some sort of law about people knowing these things about one of their parents?

My mother finally shuts up as Jim leads the group in a toast that consists of everyone raising their shot glasses, chanting "Tee Time, Tee Time, Tee Time!" before downing the whiskey.

Carter quickly learns the ins and the outs of Tee Time. Basically, the person in charge (my mother) borrows the microphone from the DJ and announces when it's Tee Time. It starts off as being every twenty minutes. After the first few rounds everyone quickly forgets just how far apart Tee Time is supposed to be. Eventually, it's every ten minutes, then every five minutes, and then there is someone puking in the middle of the dance floor and the bartender is out of a job because Tee Time attendance quickly jumped from twenty people to seventy-eight people and they've taken over the bar so they can pour the shots faster.

Every single wedding I have ever attended since I was three had a Tee Time. And frankly, even some of the funerals adopted the same tradition since honoring the dead can only be accomplished with adults sitting

121

by the casket snort-laughing and loudly discussing how they think they just saw the body move.

Two hours after the first Tee Time, I plant my ass down at one of the tables, slide off my heels, and prop my feet up on a chair so I can watch Carter, Jim, and Drew attempt to break dance to a Celine Dion song. Drew has long since shed his tuxedo coat and white dress shirt, not really caring who sees the tee shirt he wore underneath that says "I'm not the groom, but I'll let you put a ring on it" with a picture of a cock ring below the words. I watch Carter attempt to do the Running Man, unable to stop the huge grin that spreads across my face.

"Good thing I caught you in a good mood," Liz states as she suddenly appears next to my chair and grabs my hand, pulling me up and out of my seat. "Get your ass up. It's bouquet-toss time."

I let go of her hand and sit right back down.

"Nice try," I say with a chuckle.

Liz moves to stand right in front of me with her hands on her hips and glares down at me.

"Don't you give me that look," I threaten. "I am not standing out there in the middle of the dance floor pretending like I give a rat's ass whether or not I catch your stupid bouquet."

All around us, single women are shoving people out of the way to make it up to the dance floor in the hopes *they* will be the chosen one: the woman deemed worthy enough and loved enough to be the next one to walk down the aisle. It doesn't matter if you have a boyfriend or not. If that bouquet filled with all of the good luck from the recently married woman arcs through the air in your direction, you are as good as wed in the eyes of everyone around you.

Even if I don't really believe in that whole thing about how if you catch the bouquet you'll be the next person to get married, I'm still not taking any chances. I had learned early on that I'm probably not a good candidate for marriage. I don't really have shining examples of success in that area. My parents have five marriages between the two of them. I share the same genes as people that stayed married because the healthcare was cheaper. And also because the one time they had made an appointment with a lawyer, eight years ago, my mother got a flat tire on the way there. She still claims it was a sign from a higher power that they shouldn't get divorced. Something about "If you love something you shouldn't set it free or you'll get down to brass tacks in your tire."

I won't admit to anyone that I've been secretly wondering what it would be like to be married to Carter. Frankly, I shouldn't even be thinking it or lightening will strike and ruin everything. Our life is perfect just the way it is. A few stray thoughts here and there about what it would be like to sign the name Mrs. Claire Ellis doesn't mean anything. It just means that every once in a while I can act like a typical girl. It doesn't mean I have any desire to don a white dress and parade myself in front of hundreds of people whose only thought about me at that moment in time is whether or not it's appropriate for me to be wearing white.

And besides, men run for the hills as soon as you get the tiniest inkling you might want to someday be married to them. If you so much as glance in the general direction of a bridal magazine in the store, they start hyperventilating and imagining balls and chains permanently secured to their legs for all of eternity. Really, I'm doing this for Carter. I'm saving him from a coronary or some other life threatening illness that comes from thinking about marriage. I think I read somewhere that just saying the word *marriage* makes a man's balls shrink. It must have been Google.

Before I know what was happening, both Jenny and Liz are dragging me onto the dance floor amid hordes of women who are foaming at the mouth and practically punting away young children who ran from their parents to join in on the game of catch.

Once I'm firmly ensconced by giddy, annoying females on all sides, Liz turns and flees the scene.

"Oh my gosh, oh my gosh, oh my gosh! I hope I catch the flowers! What if I catch the flowers? Could you imagine?! We should move closer to the front. Or maybe go to the back. Can Liz throw really far? I hope they don't get stuck in one of the chandeliers."

I cross my arms in front of me in protest and roll my eyes as Jenny's incessant chatter rings in my ears like an annoying cow bell.

"These parents need to come out here and get their kids. What happens if one of them catches the bouquet? Will someone tell them to give it back? This is like, a really important thing. They're not opposed to be out here."

I sighed and scan the crowd looking for Carter, hoping to get a smile of encouragement from him to brave this storm. He would feel my pain and know how miserable I am in this moment, surrounded by crazies.

As my eyes move through the sea of people standing around watching, Liz is handed the microphone and with her back to the single women, she begins her countdown.

"5, 4, 3, 2, 1!"

Finally, my eyes lock on Carter standing not far from Liz. The corners of my mouth begin curling up when a sudden blur of activity around me causes my focus to wane. Heels are flying, taffeta is swirling, and women are going down like dominoes. I unfold my arms to move away from the chaos when the bouquet Liz throws drops down into my hands like a gift from the heavens.

All movement on the floor around me stops and the pile of wrestling women stare up at me with reverence like I hold the Holy Grail in my palms. I have the strongest urge to spike it to the ground like a football and get as far away from it as possible.

I don't know what scared me more. The fact that the impulse to get rid of the bouquet disappears as quickly as it comes and I find myself cradling the flowers like a baby out of fear that someone will try to take them from me, or the look of sheer horror on Carter's face when my eyes find his again.

14. PORN AND SNOZZBERRIES

My best friend has been gone on her honeymoon for a week and I feel lost. I need someone to talk to. I'm sure I could have called her if it was an emergency, but trying to explain to her that I think Carter thinks I want to get married and I think it's got him freaked out while she's lying on a beach in Maui would probably be wrong.

"Hey, Liz! How's the honeymoon? Oh that's wonderful! Speaking of wonderful, I think Carter is afraid I want to get married, so I've been trying to let him know I don't really want to get married when secretly it's all I can think about but it scares the holy fucking hell out of me."

Yeah, that makes perfect sense.

All I've been able to think about for the past few days is the look on Carter's face when I catch the bouquet. He looks like he did the day he met Gavin and got kicked in the nuts. And who knows what the hell *my* problem is. Suddenly I'm crying during an episode of *"A Wedding Story"* on TLC and thinking the bride is totally justified in refinancing her house to pay for a third wedding dress with the Swarovski crystals on *"Bridezillas"*.

I had woke up the other day at four in the morning because I didn't want Carter to know I set the DVR so I could see if the girl from New Jersey on *"My Fair Wedding"* let her fiancé dress up like a Yeti and sing John Denver songs at the rehearsal dinner. Carter came home from work a few minutes early and I jumped up from the couch in shock and turned off the television as fast as I could.

"Hey, what are you doing up?" Carter asked. He set his work bag down on the floor and walked over to the middle of the living room to pick up the blanket I dumped on the floor in my haste to shut off the TV.

"Um...uh...nothing. I wasn't watching anything," I stammered, looking nervously back and forth between the TV and Carter.

He raised an eyebrow at me and looked down at the remote in my hand where my finger was still poised above the power button.

His eyes slowly moved back up to my face that was now covered in a thin sheen of sweat from my nerves going haywire. I could feel my cheeks heating up and knew he must be wondering why they were turning red if I had nothing to hide.

He was going to know I recorded *"Say Yes to the Dress: Atlanta"*. I couldn't just be happy with Kleinfeld's. Oh no, I had to get greedy and see what people bought from Bridals by Lori.

Carter turned to look at the TV again and then back to me, his eyes suddenly going wide.

"Oh my gosh. Claire, were you watching-"

"No!" I interrupted him. "I wasn't watching anything."

I laughed nervously and looked down at the remote in my hand, chucking it onto the couch so fast you would have thought it burned me.

"Holy hell...yes you were," he said as he stared at me in awe.

I had no idea what was going on but if he was this happy that he caught me watching the wedding channel then maybe we didn't have as big a problem as I thought.

"It's okay. You don't have to be embarrassed. It's actually kind of hot."

I looked at Carter like he was insane. And maybe he was. Maybe working all these late nights finally got to him. While I stood there half awake in my yoga pants and tank top, hair all askew, face flushed and embarrassed, he stared me up and down like he wanted to devour me. I had started to ask him what he was talking about and why he was looking at me that way when it had suddenly occurred to me. Four in the morning and I had been sitting in the living room under a blanket all alone looking like I just had a very fulfilling romp in the hay...with myself.

"OH MY GOD! You think I was watching-"

"Honey, really, it's fine! You don't have to be freaked out. Everyone watches a little porn now and then. I just wish you would have waited for me," he said with a leer.

So there's that. My boyfriend thinks I'm a closet porn watcher, that I sit alone in the dark while he's at work every night watching Skinemax and diddling myself. There's something wrong with me if I'd rather he think I had a porn addiction than a deep seeded need to find out if David Tutera could turn a camo, guns, and ATV wedding into a masterpiece.

To try and deter him from my fake inclination toward porn benders, alone in the dark on the couch, and to try and erase the memory in my mind of the sheer look of terror on his face at Liz and Jim's wedding when I had caught the bouquet, I've decided reverse psychology is the best route to go. It works well on kids. And men are pretty much giant babies most of the time anyway, so I figure I've got a fighting chance at getting things back to normal between us. Ever since the wedding he's gone back to being on edge and jittery around me. I think he's afraid he's going to wake up one morning strapped to the bed in a tux with me standing over him in a wedding dress, waving a sledge hammer over my head Kathy Bates-style, threatening to smash in his kneecaps if he doesn't marry me.

He should be more concerned with my father doing that, frankly.

I start off slow by telling him I absolutely don't believe that whole tradition that whoever catches the bride's bouquet is the next to marry. I believe I might have used the words *hogwash* and *twaddle* in that conversation to bring my point home. But Carter thinks I said *twat* and then it turns into an afternoon of him saying, "Twat did you say? I cunt hear you. Let's see if I can finger it out," while I try to show him just how unconcerned with this custom I am by throwing the bouquet away. The beautiful gerbera daisy, orchid, and lily nosegay that looks stunning in my hand.

Shut up. *"The Wedding Planner"* had been on the other night and Jennifer Lopez taught me what a nosegay is. I had also learned that Alex, the hot doctor from *"Grey's Anatomy"*, isn't so hot when he's playing a guy a few fries short a Happy Meal with a shitty Italian accent. And also, the guy from the Magic Bullet infomercial looks a lot like Nigel from *"So You Think You Can Dance"*. Also, late night television should be illegal in all fifty states and maybe I really would be better off watching *"Sweet Home I'll-a-Slam-Ya"* or *"Driving Into Miss Daisy"*.

"Claire, what the hell is your problem? You've been moping around all day," Jenny says as she comes out of the office of the shop with some invoices for me to sign in her hand.

I jump at the sound of her voice and realize I've been dipping the same pretzel in chocolate for the past twenty minutes.

Liz might not be here, but at least I have *someone* to bounce my thoughts off of.

"Carter thinks I have a porn addiction," I blurt out.

"Ooooooh me too!" she replies with glee.

My mouth dropped opens and I stare at her in shock.

"Oh no! I don't mean I think *you* have a porn addiction. Well, not that I know of. I mean Drew thinks *I* have a porn addiction too. We're like twinsies!"

Yeah, I don't think so.

"I have a membership to a porn-of-the-month club. It's kind of like a jelly-of-the-month club except you don't get jelly. And I can't tell my mom about it. The porn, not the jelly. She likes jelly so I could tell her about that. I just got *'Weapons of Ass Destruction'* and *'Forest Hump'. Sex is like your box on my cock-o-late,"* she says in her best Forest Gump voice. "We should totally watch that one together!"

Not gonna happen.

"Awww, you miss Liz, don't you? I know what will cheer you up. I'm going to call Drew and have him come up and help you frost all those cookies for the baby shower order tomorrow. He took the night off of work tonight, but we don't have any plans. Did I tell you his mom's been making these amazeball cookies for his sick uncle and the guy just raves about them and keeps asking for more? I'll have Drew bring some up so you can try them. Maybe they'll spark a little creative genius in you. You can put us to work, kick back, relax, and enjoy someone else's cookies for once," Jenny rambles as she pulls out her cell phone and starts dialing. "Don't forget you have that interview with *'The Best of Baking'* magazine so we can go over some things for that while we're at it."

Even though I'm now privy to more of Jenny and Drew's sex life than I ever wanted to be and the sound of her voice droning on is starting to give me a headache, I have to admit that hiring her to help out with all my back office stuff was a stroke of brilliance. She had secured me my own domain name instead of a website that included the words "freesite4everyone" in the address, and once I forbid Drew from sneaking in thumbnail pictures of his penis in the "about me" section, it actually looked very professional. Customers can place orders online and even print out coupons thanks to Jenny. She's organized my schedule so I can work around Gavin's three days of preschool a week and see Carter before he leaves for work every day, and she's managed to get me an in-studio interview with the local news station and three write-ups in local baking magazines; the first of which is scheduled for tomorrow.

In just a few days, my best friend will be home from her honeymoon, and I'll be able to get her advice about Carter. I am so worried about saying or doing something to scare him away that I might have taken it to the extreme. When he had asked me this morning if I wanted more cream for my coffee I replied, "Speaking of cream. Why do women wear cream to their wedding? Weddings are stupid. Married people are stupid. I think I broke my thumb."

No, I don't know why the fuck I told him I thought I broke my thumb. I had panicked. And now I'm pretty sure he thinks my maybe-broken-thumb is due to the late night pornography habit I just can't quit and it's either from A) pressing the rewind and or pause buttons too quickly or B) pressing MY buttons too quickly. Either option is not something I care for him to be wondering about me every time he looks in my general direction.

I spend the rest of the afternoon trying to think of ways to convince Carter I'm not going to pressure him into marriage while at the same time making sure I don't look like I need thirty days in a Betty Ford Triple X Clinic. I've been trying to come up with new ideas for things I can cover in chocolate for the shop. The chocolate covered potato chips and crushed pretzels mixed together had been a huge hit and are one of the main attractions lately. I want something fun and new to talk about in the magazine interview the next morning, so I put all thoughts of doom aside and concentrate on what I do best. For once, I'm not dreading a visit from Drew. With his appetite, I'm sure we could come up with something spectacular.

~

"These snozzberries taste like SNOZZBERRIES!" I yell.

In the far recesses of my mind, I realize I was licking a scratch-n-sniff chocolate-covered strawberry sticker that Jenny had affixed to my shirt, but I don't care.

It smells like it tasty smells. Like snozzberries in a mountain of sticker glue. Why don't more people eat glue? It's delicious. Snozzberries should be our national fruit.

"I should cover these stickers in chocolate and sell them," I mumble as I continue swiping my tongue along the bottom hem of my shirt that I hold up by my mouth.

Drew laughs and I stop the manic sticker-licking to glance up at him. I blink really hard and try to get him to come into focus but it's not working. It's like I'm looking at him through a pair of binoculars backward. He's really small and really, really far away. I can feel my head swaying from side to side and I keep making my eyes open really wide in an effort to see more clearly. It's not working. Take your hand and make a fist then hold it up to one eye. Open your hand just enough to let some light in and that's the view I have right now.

Maybe that's what the problem is. There's someone walking around next to me holding their fists in front of my eyes.

I start flailing my arms all around my head to smack the hidden fists away until I start running into things and knocking shit off of the counters. I'm seventy-four percent positive the noise I make while doing this scares those assholes with their sneaky fists away.

"This chocolate is burning my hand! HOLY FUCK IT'S BURNING! WHY IS IT BURNING?!"

If I squint I can kind of see that Drew is holding his hand out from his body and it was dripping with hot, melted chocolate.

"Your hand looks delicious," I tell him as I absently bring my shirt back up to my mouth and began chewing on it.

"This was the best idea EVER," Jenny states as she helps Drew hold his chocolate hand over the sink so it won't drip on the floor. "Everyone will love chocolate-covered Drew. Make sure you tell them during the interview that this was my idea. I want street cred for it."

I feel my head bobbing up and down in agreement and watch the room go in and out of focus and wonder why the walls are moving closer to me all of a sudden. I look down and my feet aren't moving. I look back up and scream because the wall is right against my nose.

HOW THE FUCK DID THE WALL GET ON MY NOSE?!

"Claire, stop sniffing the wall. It doesn't have any flavor left," Jenny tells me.

Stupid wall. It runs out of flavor too fast.

I step away from the wall and look up at the ceiling. There are marshmallows on my ceiling.

Marshmallows is a funny word.

"Mmmmmmaaaaaarrrrrsssssshhhhhhmmmmaaaa lllloooowwwwsssss. Who invented that word? It's a great word. I wonder if they used to be called something else. Like *shmashmoos*. But people couldn't say shmashmoos and babies were crying because they really wanted shmashmoos but couldn't say the word and their mothers kept giving them cookies when all they really wanted were shmashmoos. Babies were crying, parents were crying, the streets were filled with people who just wanted shmashmoos. Total anarchy, dudes. I bet that was the real reason for World War II. It's one big shmashmoo conspiracy the government doesn't want us to know about."

"Claire, you are so smart," Jenny tells me seriously.

"I know, right?"

I should light a fire and make S'mores.

"Quick, someone get me a lighter, STAT!" I yell.

Drew jumps down off of the counter and with one hand, pulled his cell phone out of his pocket and started fiddling with the buttons while he holds his chocolate hand out from his body.

"Are you calling the cops? Oh shit! JENNY RUN! IT'S THE FUZZ!" I yell as I run in circles around the kitchen island.

Somewhere in the distance I hear Jenny crying. At least I think it' Jenny crying. It might have been me.

Am I crying? My face does feel kind of weird and wet. Like a wet fish.

"Give me that fiiiiish. Give me that Filet-a-Fish fiiiiish, ooooh!"

I wish McDonald's delivered. I want some ketchup.

Drew steps into my path and I slam into him. He shoves his phone in my hand and smiles. "You're welcome. Now get in that kitchen and make me some S'mores, beotch!"

I clutch the phone to my chest and look up to thank him. But he isn't up anymore, he's down. Down, down, down like a tiny little dwarf. I squint and bend down so I can see him better. He's jumping up and down, and I'm pretty sure he's trying to bite my ankles. He's like a little chocolate covered munchkin from the Land of Oz and he's angry.

Why are munchkins so angry all the time? They're in a club called the Lollipop Guild. The mother fucking Lollipop Guild! All lollipops all the time. Munchkins are ungrateful little bastards. Those lollipops died so you could be happy. RESPECT THE LOLLIPOP!

"What in the mother fucking of all fucks happened here?" Carter asks as he steps into the kitchen of the shop.

"Oh shit, the jig is up! HIDE THE COOKIES!" Drew yells as he belly flopped onto the floor and army crawls away as fast as he could.

15. JUST SAY NO TO NECROPHILIA

When my foreman had told me I could take the night off, I didn't even take a breath or say a word to anyone. My work bag is slung over my shoulder and I'm racing through the plant before the guy even finishes his sentence. Being two people short, with Jim still on his honeymoon and Drew taking a vacation day, it's a rare thing to still have enough people to send someone home. There is no way I'm going to give anyone a chance to change their minds. All I can think about is going to see Claire.

Too many thoughts have been running through my head all week and I just want to put my arms around her and get some reassurance that everything is okay between us. She's been saying some really strange things ever since Liz and Jim's wedding, and I can't stop thinking about them.

Does she really think marriage is stupid? Maybe her idea of happiness isn't settling down with someone for the rest of her life. It's not like her parents have given her any kind of good examples of finding the one you're meant to be with and spending forever loving them. They change spouses more than Drew changes his underwear. But I see her get misty eyed more than once while watching a wedding or a proposal on television when she thinks I'm not looking so I don't think she's completely opposed to the concept.

Shit, maybe it's just *me* she opposed to. Maybe she just doesn't want to marry *me.* The thought makes me sick to my stomach. Everything about her makes me happier than I have ever been in my life. Becoming a father overnight is something I never thought I wanted but now know I can never live without. Ever since the wedding this past weekend, all I can think about is the way Claire looked standing in the middle of the dance floor holding that bouquet of flowers she had just caught.

There had been a sparkle in her eyes and a smile on her face that lit up the room. It made me wish that it was *our* wedding we were at and that it was *our* celebration of love. I actually reached into my pocket to pull out the ring I always carried with me and panicked when I didn't feel it in there. It took me a minute to realize I decided right before we walked out of the house that morning to leave it at home. I had been to enough weddings with Drew to know that there would be break dancing and tuxedo jackets swung around and didn't want to chance losing the ring. After the way she reacted when she only *thought* Drew and Jenny might be getting engaged at the rehearsal dinner, I was glad I'd left the ring at home. Standing there and staring at her with a wedding bouquet in her hand had almost forced me to do something she'd hate, and I'd have no control over if that ring was in my pocket.

Claire seems genuinely happy, aside from the past few days and the weird, off-the-wall comments she makes about marriage. Could it be that seeing her best friends get married has made her realize she'll never have that for herself? She's watching porn in the middle of the night by herself while I'm at work. That's either the sign of the apocalypse or I'm just not doing it for her. Jesus, maybe I need to up my game. She shouldn't be watching porn alone unless I'm not enough for her.

Am I not enough for her? WHY AREN'T I ENOUGH FOR HER? Why can't she be happy with me instead of lusting after some actor on the television? Why, God, why? It's not like those men are real anyway. Everything about them is fake, including their six pack abs and horse cocks. And seriously, who needs that much cock? Maybe she's watching those men wishing I could learn some of those tricks. But come on, give me a break. No one is that bendy or has that much stamina. That's what film editing is for. She probably thinks it's not cheating since all she's doing is watching them on TV but God dammit, she's cheating with her MIND.

Oh my Jesus. I think I just grew a vagina.

I have to believe that if Claire is really that unhappy with me or my sexual prowess, she'd say

135

something. Chicks like to tell you all the time what you're doing wrong, don't they? Why would Claire be any different? I'm acting like a giant pussy over this. We're fine, she's fine, I love her more than anything in the world, and I WILL make this proposal happen. Enough with the chicken shit stuff.

I try calling Claire on the way out of work to see if she's still at the shop but her phone goes straight to voicemail. When I drive through town I see that her car is still parked out in front of the building, so I pull around back and go in through the back door that brings me into the kitchen.

The sight before me leaves me speechless and confused. I really don't' know where to look first. There is chocolate splattered everywhere and as I take a step into the room, something covered in chocolate dripped down from the ceiling in front of me and lands by my foot with a *plop.*

It's dead silent in the room which is my first clue that something is off; Claire always has music playing in the kitchen when she works.

Actually, my first inclination that something isn't quiet right is seeing Jenny sitting in the sink crying. My eyes pass right over Drew lying on his stomach on the floor lapping up a puddle of chocolate like a dog. That's not something I haven't seen before unfortunately.

Since Jenny is closest to me, I start with her.

"Hey, what's going on? Why are you crying? More importantly, why are you crying in the sink?" I ask her as I reach in and scoop her out of the big, stainless steel commercial sink like a baby. It takes a few minutes to steady her once I get her on her feet. She clutches onto my shoulders and stares up at me.

"I think Drew ate Claire," she whispers. "She was sitting here a minute ago and then Drew said he was hungry and now she's gone. He ate four batches of chocolate chip cookies and one batch of Claire."

Jesus God what the fuck is going on?

I gently push Jenny away from me until her back is leaning up against the counter and I am certain she won't fall. Turning around, I stare at the mess that has transformed this sparkling clean kitchen into a chocolate nightmare.

Are those chocolate covered Twinkies stuck to the wall?

I gingerly step around small puddles of melted chocolate on the floor, careful not to slip and fall, and make my way over to Drew who has given up sucking chocolate off of the floor and is now curled up in the fetal position asleep.

"Hey, ASSHOLE!" I yell. "Wake up!" I shove the toe of my shoe into his stomach and push until he rolls over onto his back and lazily opens his eyes to look at me.

"Duuuuuuuuuude," he says on an exhale of breath.

"Don't *dude* me. What the fuck happened here? Claire sent me a text a few hours ago that you were going to help her frost cookies. Why does it look like a bomb exploded?"

Drew blinks a few times and shakes his head to clear out the cobwebs or whatever the fuck is in his brain right now sucking out all of the functioning parts.

"Help me up so I can think," Drew says as he sticks his arm up towards me.

I shake my head in annoyance, grab onto his hand and yank him up off of the floor.

"You're hands are so soft. Do you moisturize?" Drew questions as he pets the top of my hand like a kitten.

I rip my hand out of his grip and smack him upside the head.

"Cocksucker! Pay attention!"

Drew rubs the back of his head and glares at me.

"Don't get your panties all in a twist. Claire is in her office. She's fine. Her dad is in there with her."

Okay, so it can't be that bad if George is here.

I leave Drew with Jenny so I can go in search of Claire. Jenny isn't going to stop crying until she sees Claire with her own eyes and realizes she hasn't been eaten.

137

Only in MY life would those words make perfect sense.

Claire and Liz share an office and it is situated right in the middle of their connecting stores. They each have a door that leads into the office. It's really no bigger than a walk-in closet. It houses a computer table and chair, a loveseat, and two metal filing cabinets. I walk over to the closed door and press my ear against it trying to figure out if Claire and her father are in some deep discussion while all hell breaks loose in her kitchen. I'm pretty sure her father still plots fun and exciting ways to kill me so there is no way I'm going to interrupt them if that's the case. I don't hear anything so I turn the knob and slowly open the door.

I had to do a double-take when I see George curled up in a ball on the loveseat. How he had managed to get his six foot frame wedged in between the arms of that thing I will never know. I decide to let sleeping dogs lie for the moment and turn in a full circle, my eyes finally coming to rest on Claire.

She's sitting on the floor behind the door with her knees pulled up to her chest. She has a spatula in one hand held out from her body with chocolate frosting dripping off of it and what looks like Drew's iPhone pressed up against the wall with her other hand. Her eyes are glassy and vacant as she stares off into space, never once blinking as I walk up to her and crouch down in front of her.

I don't know what I'm dealing with here so I speak in a soft, calming voice. "Hey there, Claire. How are you doing sweetie?"

She moans in response, but still doesn't blink.

I look over my shoulder and see George is still fast asleep. Obviously he isn't going to be any help here.

"Can you tell me what happened here tonight?"

Another moan coupled with a bit of a whimper. Still no blinking.

How long can someone go without blinking before they go blind?

138

I feel like I walked into a horror movie and found the sole survivor of a serial killer rampage. I'm afraid to say the wrong thing for fear I'll spook her and will never get to the bottom of the truth.

"I ate cookies," she finally mutters.

"Wow, that's great, sweetie," I tell her kindly.

I don't really know if that's great or not but at least she has ingested something that will sop up whatever it is that's turned these guys into chocolate covered zombies.

"I don't want to feel this anymore," she says in a pitiful voice. "Make it stop."

Maybe I should try and get her to throw up. Should I stick my fingers down her throat? I've never done that before. Not even to myself. I've only ever tried to make Drew throw up, and usually all I have to do is talk about his grandmother having sex.

I reach over and take the dripping spatula out of her hand and set it on the floor. I do the same with Drew's cell phone, flipping it over first and noticing it's set to the BIC Lighter app, the fake flame flickering back and forth on the screen.

"Honey, why are you holding Drew's phone against the wall?"

"I wanted to make hot. Stupid fight wouldn't lire. Flight wouldn't flier. Fire wouldn't fire. Fire. Fire, fire, fire, fire, fire-"

Sweet Jesus.

I slide an arm between Claire's back and the wall and bring her forward so she's leaning over her bent knees. Hoping she won't hate me for this or bite me, I push my finger passed her lips and into her mouth. She blinks then and looks up at me, trying to focus on my face. My finger is in her mouth but she won't open her lips, they just stay wrapped around my finger while she squints and tries to see me better.

I wiggle my hand and try to push my finger in further. Her throat has to be in there somewhere. If I can just get back there far enough I'm sure she will puke.

"Come on, Claire. Open up wider. I can't get it in."

I grunt with the effort of holding her up and trying to get the knuckle of my first finger past her teeth.

"Don't bite me. You'll feel much better after this is done, I promise. I've done this a bunch of times, just let me in."

Either she isn't hearing me or she doesn't care. I move my hand around her mouth and try every angle I can but she just won't open her mouth so I could reach her throat. Her tongue presses against the tip of my finger preventing it from moving.

"Claire, don't be difficult," I groan. "I need to do this deeper."

Claire bites down on my finger at the same time I feel a hand slap down on my shoulder.

I yank my finger out of her mouth and whip my head around and up to find George towering over me with his hands on his hips and a glare on his face.

"Carter," George greets.

"Hi, Mr. Morgan," I say as cheerfully as possible, considering he's looking at me like I'm a bug he's getting ready to squash under his shoe.

"Have you seen my shotgun?" he asks.

I gulp loudly and try to remember all of the reasons it would be bad to piss my pants right then. Under normal circumstances, I'm quite used to the death stares and silent threats I receive from Claire's dad, but this seems a little excessive. I'm trying to save his daughter's life. How can he possible be angry with me about that? He had been asleep on the couch two seconds ago. He must have opened his eyes and seen me...

You'll feel much better once this is done. Don't be difficult, I need to do this deeper. Just let me in...

Oh sweet Jesus. He had probably looked across the room and saw just the back of me trying to force something in his daughter's mouth.

Why the hell couldn't Rachel have been the one here tonight? She would have woken up and cheered me on, probably even booing me when she found out I was only trying to make her daughter puke instead of forcing my penis in her mouth.

"I am NOT into Necrophilia," I state firmly to him.

"There is something wrong with you," he mutters.

"I just wanted her to throw up," I complain.

"I really don't want to know about the weird, kinky shit you're into."

"Yo, Mr. Morgan, you're awake!" Drew exclaims as he lounges in the doorway. "And Carter, dude, it's called *Poutiphilia.* You just told Claire's dad you weren't into banging dead people. Which is a good thing, but probably not what you were going for. Poutiphilia is a person who enjoys sexual relations with people who are passed out."

Drew is a walking, talking Urbandictionary dot com.

"I was NOT trying to have sexual relations with this woman!" I shout.

"Slow your roll there, Clinton," Drew says as he came further into the room and squats down next to me.

"HOW ARE YOU DOING, CLAIRE?" Drew yells, talking to her slow and loud like she doesn't understand English. "DO YOU KNOW WHO I AM?"

He snaps his fingers in front of her face a few times. She finally blinks and looks up at me.

"Make it stop," she whines.

I'm not sure if she is referring to Drew or whatever is in her system. I decide to err on the side of caution and punch Drew in the arm.

"What the fuck did you give her?"

"Just some cookies. My mom makes them for my uncle all the time and he loves them," Drew tells me.

"Did you guys get food poisoning or something? Why the hell is this place such a disaster and Claire is almost comatose?"

I briefly wonder if I should try again to make her puke, but I'm a little afraid George really does have a shotgun hidden somewhere in the room.

"Claire wanted some help coming up with some new ideas for things to cover in chocolate. It was a process. A *creative* process. You wouldn't understand. It's an artistic thing," Drew explains. "Chocolate covered carrots were a bust, but we might have something with chocolate covered gummy bears."

This still doesn't make any sense. I'm obviously missing something.

"So you guys ate some cookies and brainstormed. What kind of cookies did you eat? Were they undercooked?"

Maybe Claire has Salmonella poisoning. Is that contagious? Does she need to be vaccinated or have her stomach pumped? I feel like I should know the answer to this since I have a kid. What if Gavin eats some raw chicken and I don't know whether to give him mouth-to-mouth or Pepto Bismol? Is he even allowed to have Pepto? And where the fuck is he getting raw chickens from?!

"Dude, I'm not Betty fucking Crocker or anything. I don't know what was in the cookies. They were mocha coffee nut something or other. Wait, maybe it was the nuts. Is Claire allergic to nuts? She might be going into anal flaccid shock," Drew says nervously.

Oh my God. It's like he shares a brain with Jenny.

"It's Anaphylaxis Shock, dumbass, and no, she's not allergic to nuts," I say with a roll of my eyes.

"My uncle begs my mom for these cookies. Seriously. They actually STOP him from getting sick so this makes absolutely no sense. My mom makes them for him every couple of weeks before he goes in for chemo."

I stare at him blankly and repeat in my head the words that just came out of his mouth just to make sure I'm not hallucinating.

"Jesus fucking Christ! You gave her POT COOKIES???

I whip my head around and stare at George in disbelief.

"YOU ate a pot cookie?" I ask incredulously.

"I was in Nam," he huffs like that's sufficient enough evidence this is perfectly okay. "Where's my grandson?"

I stare at him in wonder for a few minutes, realizing (not for the first time) that Claire's father is the epitome of the saying "The man, the myth, the legend". While everyone else has been one step away from bath-salts-crazy, George has curled up on the couch and slept off his pot cookie high.

"Gavin is with my parents for the night. They're in town for a wedding and are keeping him overnight at their hotel so he can swim in the pool," I explain as I tighten my hold on Claire and help her stand up.

"I'm hungry," Claire announces to no one in particular as she suddenly regains the use of all of her faculties and pushes away from me. Her eyes are bright and clear as she walks out of the office, squeezing her way past Drew, like nothing is wrong.

"Well, it looks like the problem is solved thanks to me. Claire now has a new item to put on her menu and rave about tomorrow during her magazine interview," Drew states proudly.

"She's not putting pot cookies on the menu," I tell him with a shake of my head as we all amble out of the office. "It's illegal."

"You're a real buzz kill, you know that?" Drew complains.

143

16. SON OF A FACE TURD

"I eat my poop."

"Drew, I swear to God if you don't stop playing with that fucking computer, I'm going to shove it up your ass," I threaten as I finished chiseling the last bit of chocolate off of the walls of the shop kitchen.

Drew has recently learned how to turn on text-to-speech in Microsoft Excel. Everything he types into a box on the spreadsheet is repeated back to him in a computerized voice. He had stopped by my shop first thing this morning under the guise of helping me clean but instead has spent the majority of his time making the computer say random, stupid shit.

"I like to touch boobs," the monotone, computerized voice announces.

"Boobs, boobs, boobies, boobs. I like boobies."

Drew sticks his head out of my office a few seconds later and smiles.

"Claire Bear, do you have a pot hangover?"

I growl as I throw the dirty rag into the sink and turn on the tap to wash my hands of the sticky mess they'd become since I started cleaning up the mess we made of the kitchen the previous night.

"After what you did to me last night, you're lucky I'm not shoving a spatula in your eye.

I turn off the water and dry my hands on the towel next to the sink. When I look back over my shoulder to throw another insult at Drew, he isn't there.

"Claire has an angry vagina."

I roll my eyes and take one last look around the kitchen to make sure I haven't missed a spot. In hindsight, I should know better than to eat anything Drew gives me. He always looks guilty and says stupid shit though, so when he hands me the cookie and tells me to "Eat the entire thing or else," I don't think twice. All I had wanted was a nice, quiet evening of brainstorming and keeping my mind off of anything to do with weddings and marrying the man of my dreams.

Be careful what you wish for.

144

I had woken up this morning with a sinking feeling in the pit of my stomach that I did something stupid. I rolled over and found Carter sitting on the edge of the bed staring at me.

"I was just getting ready to stick a mirror under your nose to make sure you were still breathing," Carter said with a laugh as he stood up from the bed and walked over to the dresser to put on his watch and stick his wallet in his back pocket.

"What the fuck did I do last night?" I groaned with a raspy, morning after voice.

"Which part exactly are you referring to? Eating an entire pot cookie or redecorating the shop by painting the walls with chocolate?"

"Okay, first of all, I didn't KNOW it was a pot cookie until after I took the first bite and second…I don't know. I have no excuse for the rest of it," I trailed off.

"If you knew it was a pot cookie after the first bite, why in the hell would you keep eating it?" Carter asked with a chuckle as I scooted up in bed until I could sit against the headboard.

"Why wouldn't I eat it? The damage was already done. And it was a delicious cookie."

Carter shook his head at me and sighed.

"Claire, you are only supposed to eat a little bit of a pot cookie, never the entire thing at once."

He stared at me like I was an idiot and this was clearly something everyone knew.

"How in the fuck am I supposed to know something like that? Do I look like the type of person who goes around eating pot cookies all the time?" I asked angrily.

"Everyone knows this. I've never eaten a pot cookie, and I still know the rules."

"The rules? Is there a Pot Cookie 101 class I missed or something? It's not like the fucking thing came with an owner's manual. I was handed a cookie, and I ate a cookie. Who in their right mind only takes one bite of a cookie and then puts the rest back for later?" I demanded.

145

"Someone who eats a pot cookie," Carter deadpanned.

After I had showered and dressed, I left the house with an obvious bug up my ass.

And now my magazine interview is in an hour and the only things surrounding me are bad, hallucinogenic ideas – chocolate covered gummy bears, pickles, moon pies, M&M's, every Little Debbie snack treat imaginable from Twinkies to Swiss Rolls, and a computer printed picture of Drew's hand covered in chocolate. Trays of chocolate covered crap litter the counters, and I berate myself for all of those hours we spent NOT coming up with a good idea. At least Drew manages to frost all two-hundred cookies for the order that's being picked up today. It makes my hatred for him go down just a tiny bit.

"The peanut butter on your cock is delicious."

"DREW!" I yell again in warning.

"Sorry!" he yells back, trying to mask his giggles.

"Cock, the other white meat."

I open my mouth to scream another threat at Drew, this one to his manhood, when an idea strikes.

I glance at the clock and quickly rush around the kitchen, grabbing the ingredients I need. While I wait for the chocolate to melt, I grab a small, white packaging box from under the counter. I prepare it by adding a sheet of pink tissue paper inside to line the box and affix a "Seduction and Snacks" sticker to the outside. I watch the clock out of the corner of my eye as I get down to business, crossing my fingers, toes, and even my legs that this idea would work.

Thirty minutes later I finish placing the last of the new candy inside the box, seal the lid closed, tie a neat, pink and white ribbon around it, and grab my purse from under the counter.

"Drew, I'm leaving. Don't forget to go next door and wait for Liz's delivery so you can sign for it," I yell to him as I head to the front door to make sure the "Closed" sign is in place. I have about twenty minutes now to run home, pick up Gavin, and drive to the meeting spot. The magazine adamantly insists that I bring Gavin with me. This magazine interviewes people due to customer recommendations. Customers write into the magazine and suggest businesses they believe should be spotlighted for one reason or another.

The magazine had done some research, made some calls, and for whatever reason decided "Seduction and Snacks" needed a write up. When the magazine called to set up the interview, they told Jenny that the customers raved not only about the sweets we sold but also about the owner's mouthy little son that ran around the store and made everyone laugh. It had been a toss-up on whether or not I should be horrified by this or happy that Gavin's penchant for swear words and constant talk about his wiener was finally doing something good in the world.

It's still hard to wrap my head around the fact that our businesses had taken off so quickly. Never underestimate the need for sugar and sex in small-town-America. With one last look around the darkened store to make sure everything is in order, I step outside to the faint sound of the computer speaking one last Drew-initiated command.

"Son of a face turd, you whore. Touch my taint and tickle my balls."

~

I walk into Playland McDonalds with butterflies flapping in my stomach and my hand clutched tightly around Gavin's.

I don't know why I'm so nervous. I've done a few phone interviews since we opened and those had been a piece of cake. Maybe it's the fact that I've never done something like this with my son right next to me - my lovely son who likes to talk to random strangers about his poop.

This will be fine. No big deal. Just a couple of questions. Easy peasy.

"Remember, best behavior," I remind Gavin as we make our way through the crowded restaurant to a

147

booth in the back. I can see the interviewer already seated with her laptop open on the table. We make eye contact and she gives me a wave.

"I want to play in the playland," Gavin whines.

"You will, as soon as the interview is over."

"That's dumb," he mutters.

"Too bad. Be good and you can get a Happy Meal."

"Can I have pop too?" he asks.

I pause, contemplating his request. Being a parent is tough, especially when it comes to negotiations. You don't want your kids to think they can have whatever they ask for, but you also don't want them to tell the interviewer of a national magazine that their nuts smell like cheese and it's because she's so ugly. Pick your battles, people.

"Yes, you can have pop. If you're good."

We arrive at the table and introductions are made. I direct Gavin in first so he can sit by the window and then slide in next to him.

"Hi, Gavin, my name is Lisa. I love your shirt," the interviewer from *The Best of Baking* says with a smile.

Gavin looks down at the shirt Drew had bought him a few weeks ago. It's black and in white writing reads, "Parental Advisory: Lock up your daughters."

He just shrugs in response, and I resist the urge to shoot him the evil eye and remind him to be good.

"This is just going to be an informal type of interview," Lisa explains. "I just want to ask some questions and chit chat. Just pretend like I'm one of your girlfriends."

She has a huge smile on her face like I totally understand what she's talking about. She obviously has never met my girlfriends. We don't sit around in dresses, sipping daintily from glasses of champagne while we politely discuss politics. We chug beers, do shots, and call each other thunder cunts.

I slide the white box across the table towards her, figuring I might as well start right off the bat with the bribery.

148

Lisa's eyes light up when she sees the white box with our signature pink ribbon around it.

"Oh my goddness, you brought me chocolate!" she exclaims.

"It's something new I'm trying out. I crumble up crispy bacon and mix it with white chocolate. The clusters are drizzled with caramel and butterscotch. They're called Bacolate Bunches," I tell her.

She tears into the box and takes a bite out of one of the clusters. She moans and groans and sighs for so long it gets a little uncomfortable. I'm now privy to what Lisa sounds like when she has sex. Awkward. But at least she likes my spur of the moment candy invention.

"So, Gavin, how are you doing today?" Lisa asks after she finishes the chocolate and finally gets down to business.

"I wanna play, this is boring," he complains while staring longingly at the other children who are running and screaming around the play area.

"Gavin, be nice," I warn under my breath with clenched teeth and a smile on my face for Lisa.

"Oh, it's fine!" she tells me cheerfully. "I'd like to play on those toys too," she says to Gavin.

"You're too old to go on the slide. Your butt would get stuck 'cuz you're old."

With the evil eye in full force, I glare at Gavin. "If you don't watch your mouth, you're going home to take a nap," I say quietly.

"Naps can suck it," Gavin whispers as he smacks his elbows on the table and puts his chin in his hands angrily.

Obviously, he's already forgotten the Happy Meal and pop he was promised. *God, if you're listening, just help me not kill him. At least until we're home.*

"So, Claire, how's business been going at the shop?"

I stop glaring at Gavin and hope that by some super mom power he will still be able to feel my wrath floating around him and keep his mouth shut.

"Business has been going very well. I still have to pinch myself every morning when I walk into that place. I am absolutely amazed that people actually want to buy things I make," I tell her with a laugh.

I can't believe someone is interviewing me for a magazine. I'm nobody. How is this happening?

"Are you finding it hard to juggle owning a business and spending time with your family?" Lisa asks as she typed away on her laptop.

"That's the beauty of owning a business. Basically, I can do whatever I want."

Lisa laughs and continued typing.

This sort of IS like talking to one of my girlfriends. Liz never pays attention to anything I say and is always busy doing other shit when I'm pouring my heart out to her.

"Can you elaborate on that just a little bit?" she asks.

"Well, if I want Gavin to spend the day with me, he can. I don't need to find a sitter or send him to daycare when he isn't in preschool. And if I need to close up early to take him to a doctor's appointment or to go to a function at his school, I can easily do it without having to get permission from someone else or have my pay docked for missing time," I explain.

"My doctor gives me cookies and stickers. His mean nurse is a wiener face and gives me shots," Gavin adds.

Lisa chuckles, her eyes never leaving her screen as she types furiously.

Oh my God, please tell me she didn't just type the words "wiener face" in my interview.

"In just three short months of being open, Seduction and Snacks is already turning a profit. That's almost unheard of for a new, small business. What do you think is the key to this success?"

Do I look like Donald Trump?

I don't know anything about anything. I cover things in chocolate and bake cookies. The key to success is pretending like it's not really happening so that you don't freak the fuck out thinking about it.

I answer her question as best I can without looking like a clueless moron. I tell her it's all about luck and how I honestly have no idea how this happened to me.

Lisa finally takes a break from her typing to look up at me.

"It doesn't hurt to have such a famous son either, right?! Everyone I spoke with about Seduction and Snacks told me I absolutely HAD to meet the owner's son."

Oh dear God. Here we go.

"I'm almost afraid to ask what else they said about him. He's lucky he's cute or I would have put him out on the curb with the garbage years ago," I tell her as we shared a laugh.

"You shut your mouth when you're talking to me!" Gavin shouts.

I quickly reach over and cover his mouth with my hand.

I should have packed duct tape and a taser.

"If you can believe it, I've actually been asked by several customers if they could take him home. If only they knew. A marine sergeant stopped in a few days ago on his way to work and joked that he should take Gavin with him to basic training. He figured Gavin could get the men to cry faster than he ever could," I tell her.

She types with a small smile on her face, and I wonder if this will be my first and last magazine interview ever.

"As you know, we do a little research on the people we're going to interview. Being from a small town, it's no secret that you got pregnant and had to drop out of college. It's a huge struggle to be a single mother. What advice do you have for other women who might be going through the same thing?" Lisa asks as she bends her head and goes back to clacking away at her keyboard.

Lovely. I bang a guy at a frat party, get knocked up, and have to work at a bar to make ends meet. The only other option available to me at the time had been pregnant stripping. Is this really something the people of *"The Best of Baking"* want to know? They seem like a conservative group - ones who talk about petit fours and balsamic reductions, not beer pong and vagina pounding.

"Um, yeah. I'm definitely not the best person to come to for advice in that area," I tell her honestly. "I did everything wrong. Luckily, Gavin's father is an amazing man and we were able to find our way back to one another. I honestly don't know what I would do without him. I can't imagine my life without him in it."

Shit! Can I retract that statement?! That sounds entirely too much like saying I want to spend the rest of my life with him. Which I do. But he can't know that. He'll freak out like a guy. Which he is. When he reads this, his mind is immediately going to go to marriage and he'll probably start screaming. *CHANGE THE SUBJECT, CLAIRE!*

"Also, I like to watch a lot of porn."

NO, NO, NO! ABORT MISSION! What the fuck am I supposed to be talking about? Oh, right. Advice.

"Don't look a gift horse in the mouth or he'll bite the hand that feeds you."

Oh sweet Jesus I just became my mother.

Lisa doesn't show any signs of thinking she's talking to a lunatic. She just keeps on typing. It's starting to freak me out.

Is she seriously typing every single thing I say? I suddenly have the urge to scream the words "ANAL WARTS" just to see if she keeps right on clicking away without batting an eye.

I want to ask her if she heard me say I was addicted to porn. Maybe the noise of kids playing around us or Gavin's loud huffing and sighing block out what I said. Obviously, I can't bring it up and *ask* if she heard me because if she hasn't, she'll want me to repeat it. And knowing me, I *will* repeat it to be polite and that will just fuck up this entire freak out I'm currently having.

I am hereby restricting the word "porn" from my vocabulary. It's getting me into too much trouble.

Lisa stops typing and gives me the universal one-finger, hold on a minute sign as she answers her ringing cell phone.

"Son of a bitch," I mutter.

"You said a bad word," Gavin informs me.

"I'm allowed. I'm an adult."

"I wanna be a dolt!" he says excitedly.

A few minutes later, Lisa ends her call and turns her attention to Gavin.

"How about I ask you some questions now? Would that be okay?"

"Sure," he says with a shrug.

"Do you have a nickname? Can I call you Gav?" Lisa asks.

"Can I punch you in the face?" he asks.

"Gavin!" I scold.

"What's your favorite color?" Lisa asks, both of them ignoring me.

"I like green. Green is green. I fart green."

Oh wonderful. This is turning out to be a stellar interview.

"What's your favorite food?"

"Skabetti and meat balls. Balls are delicious!" Gavin exclaims.

Lisa and I both share a snicker over that one.

"If Phineas and Ferb and Spongebob got into a fight, who would win?" Lisa questions.

Gavin thinks about this for a minute before answering.

"Spongebob 'cuz he's a big tough man. Phineas and Ferb are dumber than his wee-wee."

I roll my eyes and shake my head. This interview has officially gone in the shitter.

"What is your favorite holiday?"

"Fart."

"Gavin," I warn.

"What's your favorite animal?"

"Sheep, 'cuz they're stupid," Gavin answers with a laugh.

"What's your favorite smell?"

Oh that's a super question to ask a four-year-old who just said his favorite holiday is passing gas.

"Smelly cat. And feet," Gavin says with a giggle.

"What's your favorite song?" Lisa continues.

Please don't say "99 Problems But the Bitch Ain't One" or I will smother Carter in his sleep for downloading that to his iPod.

"SMELLY CAT, SMELLY CAT, WHAT ARE THEY FEEDING YOU!" Gavin sings as loud as he can.

"How do you even know that song?" I ask him.

Gavin replies with a shrug.

"You like to say big people words a lot. How come?" Lisa asks.

"'Cuz I like it. 'Cuz I'm a man."

"I've heard you like to talk about your wiener a lot. Why do you do that?"

'Cuz it's stupid. I crapped my pants."

Gavin laughs out loud at himself.

"Excuse me? You know you aren't supposed to say that word," I scold.

"I can't say the s-h-p word either. What the heck am I 'sposed to say?" Gavin asks with a roll of his eyes.

This is what I have to deal with. Am I supposed to correct him when he spells "shit" wrong? Why the fuck hasn't anyone printed a parenting handbook yet?

"What's your favorite thing to do?"

"Fart in everyone's face," Gavin says in between giggles. "FART!"

"You sure like to say 'fart' a lot," Lisa says with a laugh.

"'Cuz I like saying it forever, punk!"

I put my elbow on the table and my head in my hand. There is no point in even trying to put a stop to this train wreck.

"What do you like better, cookies or girls?" Lisa questions.

"My mommy makes yummy cookies. Girls are stupid. Except for Mommy 'cuz she has boobs," Gavin replies earnestly.

"Gee, thanks, sweetie," I mumble as I lift my head and glance at Lisa to see if she looks as horrified as I feel.

"When you grow up, who do you want to marry?"

Obviously, the fact that any chance at a Pulitzer for this interview is long gone doesn't matter one iota to this woman.

Gavin gets up on his knees on the bench seat and places a loud, wet kiss to my cheek.

"I want to marry Mommy. We'll kiss and we'll marry and I'll take her on dates and we'll be best friends forever and make lots of phone calls with each other."

No, no, no, no. Just...no.

"Phone calls? Do you mean you'll call your mommy a lot when you're older?" Lisa questions.

Don't do it. For the love of God, don't do it.

"No, we'll make phone calls like Mommy and Daddy do when they go into their bedroom and lock the door and yell and make weird noises," Gavin replies.

17. MIDGET AND DONKEY SHOWS

"When asked if he enjoyed preschool, the precocious four-year-old asked me if I was the police. When I told him that no, I was not the police, he informed me that I should go to jail and called me a 'dicky punk'."

Carter laughs as he reads the magazine interview aloud. Lisa had sent me an email copy of the interview right after she finished it so I could look it over, but seeing it in print in one of my absolute favorite magazines that I have read cover to cover for years and only dreamed about one day being in makes me feel a little sick to my stomach.

"How can you laugh about this? This isn't funny."

"Gavin is quite obviously fond of both of his parents. When asked what his favorite thing about his father was he replied, 'He tucks me in at night and tells me that if I eat my green beans my wiener will grow big and strong just like his,'" Carter reads with a laugh.

"I'm buying that kid a Porsche. He just told all of America that I have a big, strong penis."

I shake my head at him and get up to dump the rest of my now cold coffee into the sink and rinse out my cup. My morning coffee, which usually brings me close to orgasm and gives me the strength to make it through the day, leaves me feeling queasy. I've only been able to stomach two sips of it. I'm guessing that the combination of seeing my name in print in my most beloved food magazine and listening to Carter read back to me the embarrassment of that day three weeks ago is the culprit for my upset stomach.

"Claire, this interview is awesome. She raves about how amazing you are by making your dreams come true and how absolutely delicious everything you make is. This is going to drum up so much business for the store. You should be proud," Carter tells me. "Although, I really think we need to sit down and talk about this porn comment. I get that you're uncomfortable about it, but you don't need to be with me. I like porn. I like to watch porn. I would especially like to watch porn with you," he states as he set the magazine down on the kitchen table, stands up, and walks over to me.

He rests his hands on the counter on either side of me, caging me in. He presses his body up against my back and places a kiss to my shoulder. I sigh, memories of the last time we stood like this in the kitchen flooding my mind. Even having my mother walk in on us doesn't diminish the hotness that is kitchen sex.

"What's really going on in that head of yours?" Carter asks as he rests his chin on my shoulder and we stare out of the little window above the sink. I watch Gavin in the front yard, sitting on the walkway right in front of the porch drawing with sidewalk chalk. "I can tell something has been on your mind, so what gives?"

Just tell him. Tell him that all of a sudden after Liz and Jim's wedding, all you can think about is donning a white dress, standing in front of everyone you know, and committing the rest of your life to this man.

"Ever since the wedding you've been on edge. Don't worry, I have no intention of dragging you to the altar if that's what you're worried about," Carter says with a laugh.

I close my eyes and let my head fall forward. I should have never made those little comments all these months about how I'm not sure about the whole idea of marriage. How the hell am I supposed to know I'd change my mind?

"It's nothing, really," I reassure him, turning in his arms and putting on a happy face I don't really feel. I place my hands on his cheeks and pull his face to mine, kissing him with all of the love I feel bubbling in side of me. Carter moans softly and wraps his arms around me, holding me tight.

The front door opens and closes, and we end the kiss that's sure to heat up if we don't stop. No matter what we have going on in our minds, no matter what kind of struggles we are dealing with, nothing can change the spark between us or how much we want and need each other. That is one thing I'm absolutely positive of. Right now, that is the only thing I am sure of.

"I love you," I tell him, staring into his gorgeous blue eyes and trying to push my worries to the back of my mind. "I'm just out of sorts. Liz has been crazy busy since she got back from her honeymoon. We haven't had a lot of time to talk and I miss her. And I just haven't been feeling well."

Carter puts his hand to my forehead as Gavin comes running into the room.

"You do look a little flushed. Are you coming down with something?" he asks, pressing the back of his hand to one of my cheeks.

"I'm sure it's nothing. Just stress," I reassure him.

"Hey, Dad, guess what my favorite word is?" Gavin asks as he stands next to us, bouncing back and forth excitedly from one foot to the other.

"I don't know, what's your favorite word?" Carter asks as we separate from our embrace, and I go back to rinsing out my coffee cup and the other couple of dishes in the sink.

"Nutjob. Nutjob is my favorite word."

"Of course it is," Carter states with a sigh as he lifts Gavin into his arms and starts walking across the kitchen, no doubt to once again explain to him the difference between little people words and big people words. I know it's wrong to staple something to someone's head, but I am two seconds away from writing this rule down on a piece of paper and smacking it to Gavin's head with the black Swingline that's on our computer desk. And just that quickly, I feel like crying for even thinking about doing that to my son. I'm obviously having issues.

"I'll give Jim a call and see if they have any plans tonight. I think you just need a night out to take your mind off of everything," Carter tells me as I watch him walk out of the room giving Gavin a few tickles and blowing a zerbert on his cheek.

He's probably right. I just need a night out with friends, particularly my best friend. Liz and I haven't had any alone time since she's been home. She has told me more than once to just say the word and she'll drop everything so we can sit down and talk, but I feel bad about imposing on her. She's a newlywed with her own business to worry about. I don't want to bring her down with my insecurities. If I don't talk to someone, though, I'm going to explode. I can feel it.

Or maybe throw up. I suddenly have an image in my mind of a person literally being blown to bits with blood and gore and body parts splattering against a wall. With my hand to my mouth I race to the bathroom to throw up the small amount of coffee I consumed.

~

"Seriously, Claire? How is it that we've been friends all these months and I didn't know that you've never been to one?" Jenny asks with a shocked expression on her face.

"What are we discussing here, ladies? Donkey shows? Midget and donkey shows? Ping pong shooting vaginas in Tijuana?" Drew asks as he gets back from the bathroom and takes his seat at the table.

Carter calls everyone earlier in the day and demands they clear their schedules for a night out. It really isn't too hard to convince anyone to do this, but I still appreciate the fact that he's organized it for me and knows how much I need it. We are just finishing up dinner at Lorenzo's, our favorite local pizza place that's famous for not only good food but cheap draft beers. My stomach still isn't feeling one hundred percent better after that morning so while everyone around me enjoys their drafts, I stick to 7 Up in the hopes of settling things down.

"Claire has never been to a sex toy shop," Jenny informs him.

"Wait, I'm confused. Liz owns a sex toy shop, and it's right next door to Claire's," Drew tells her, turning his attention on me. "Dude, you've never walked over to the shop that's connected to yours? That's a little weird."

"Of course I've been to *Liz's* store. I've just never been to any other store. And I don't really think her store counts since it's not like it's full of sex toys right out in front," I explain.

"True. My store is like a mullet. Business in the front, party in the back," Liz states.

"Or like anal," Drew says with a laugh.

Everyone stares at him.

"What? It's totally like anal. Business in the front, party in the back. Hello? Why is that not funny?"

Jenny pats his arm for comfort and we all resume our discussion.

"If you guys will remember, I never even *owned* a vibrator until Liz conned me into doing one of her at-home parties," I remind them.

"Ahhhh yes, the infamous dinner where we talked about your vagina and sex toys all night long," Jim says with a laugh.

That night still goes down in history as one of the most mortifying nights of my life. It had been the night after I saw Carter again for the first time since our one-night-stand. I walked into Liz and Jim's house, talking nonsense about my vagina and how I'd never had an orgasm with another human being when I turned around and saw Carter and Drew sitting on the couch listening to every word. Jim met them earlier in the day and unbeknownst to Liz or I, invited them over for dinner. The rest of the night had been spent discussing how many sex toys I received at the party earlier that evening and the fact I only had sex one and a half times in my life.

"Anyway," I say with a glare to Jim, bringing the conversation back around. "No, I've never been inside a real, live sex toy store."

Drew pushes his chair back and stands up, placing his hands on his hips.

"Grab your keys, folks. We're going to pop Claire's toy store cherry!"

Everyone pays their bills and Liz announces to the guys that the girls need some alone time. The men all pile into Drew's car and Jenny and I get into Liz's car to head to the Adult Mart a few towns over.

"Okay, spill it bitch. What's going on with you?" Liz asks as she pulls out of the parking lot and follows Drew's car.

That's all it takes for the dam to break. I immediately start crying.

God dammit, what the fuck is wrong with me?

Jenny leans forward from the back seat and hands me a kleenex. I take it and blow my nose, taking deep breaths to calm myself down.

"I don't think Carter wants to marry me," I say between sniffles.

"Whoa, wait a minute. Did he say that to you? I will kick his fucking ass," Liz threatens as she turns on her blinker and gets onto the ramp for the highway.

"No! No, he didn't say those exact words. It's just little things that have happened the past few weeks," I tell her.

"Okay, what little things? And why is this news to me that you even care about getting married? You have always been a staunch supporter of living in sin because of your parents. Why the sudden change of heart?"

This is where I feel stupid. Does it sound dumb that my change of heart came from being jealous of her and Jim? That seeing them so happy and pledging their love to one another has made me realize how much I want that for myself?

"I know that's what I've always said, and I guess part of me really believed that. I mean come on, my parents don't exactly have the best track record. What makes me think I would be any good at that kind of thing?" I ask.

"Sweetie, no one knows if they will be good at that kind of thing. It's not like you're born with a marriage gene. It all just depends on the person you're with. If you can look at that person and know without a doubt that you want to spend the rest of your life kissing them goodnight and waking up next to them, marriage is for you," she tells me.

I start crying again and put my head in my hands.

"When I caught the bouquet at your reception, you should have seen the look of horror on Carter's face. He seriously looked petrified that the old wives' tale would come true," I explain as I wipe the tears from my cheeks and take a deep breath.

Liz stares at me while we sit at a red light.

"What?" I ask.

"You mean that's it? That's where all of this doubt and sadness is coming from? He looked at you a little funny when you caught a bouquet at a wedding? That doesn't exactly scream 'I hate marriage' you know. He could have just been a little surprised. Did he actually *say* he was freaked out that you caught the bouquet?"

I huff and my sadness is immediately replaced with irritation.

"No, he didn't come right out and say it, but I could tell. And I don't know, there's been a bunch of other little things here and there. He was all weird at your rehearsal dinner, smacking the champagne out of my hand and he's made these comments about how he won't be dragging me to the altar and how he's glad he'll never have to worry about asking my dad for permission because my dad still scares the shit out of him," I tell her.

"Um, not to butt in here or anything, but do you think maybe he's saying stuff like that because he knows how *you* feel about the whole subject? Maybe he really does want to marry you but he doesn't want to freak *you* out about the whole thing since you've made it clear your parents left a lasting impression on you in

162

that area," Jenny says from the back seat with a surprising amount of insight.

"Shockingly, I agree with Jenny. Until you sit down and talk to him about this, you're just going to keep jumping to conclusions and making yourself miserable. I love you, Claire, but you're acting like an asshole," Liz says as she pulled into the Adult Mart parking lot. "You know what happens when you assume things."

I let out a sigh. "You make an ass out of you and me."

She maneuvers the car into a spot right next to the guys and shuts off the car but makes no move to get out.

"No, you just make an ass out of *you*. Me, I would never be this assy," she replies. "You love Carter and it is obvious how much he adores you. Stop being a dick, man up, and talk to him. Sit him down and tell him that you don't really have a late night porn addiction but you've been secretly watching wedding shows and sneaking into the magazine aisle at the grocery store in sweats, slippers, sunglasses, and a trench coat to scan the bridal magazines like some deprived housewife needing a Playgirl fix," Liz tells me firmly.

"Ooooh, I love Playgirl!" Jenny said. "I have a prescription to it. I learned how to deep throat while hanging my head off of the end of the bed last month. You know how in the movie *'The 40-Year-Old Virgin'* Steve Carell screams out Kelly Clarkson's name when he's getting waxed? Drew screamed out Willie Nelson's name when he came. It was so hot."

"Oh my God, Jenny. Too much information," I tell her with a grimace as I cover my mouth with my hand and swallow back a little bit of vomit I burped up at the thought of that moment in time in Jenny and Drew's bedroom.

"Hey, are you feeling okay? You look a little green," Liz states as we opened our car doors and step out into the night air.

I take a few deep breaths and will my stomach to calm and not bring up dinner.

"And what the hell was wrong with you tonight drinking pop at Lorenzo's? That's like blasphemy," Liz tells me as she clicks the automatic door lock on her keys and the car horn beeps once. "You're not pregnant are you?!"

She and Jenny start cackling with laughter as they walk ahead of me to meet up with the guys who stand holding the door to the store open for us.

I trail behind them a few steps, the smile dying from my lips as I start doing calculations in my head. I stop in my tracks a few feet from the front door and stare in horror at Carter.

He gives me a heart-stopping smile and in response, I throw my hand over my mouth and run to the bushes on the edge of the sidewalk, depositing two slices of pizza, two glasses of pop, and my dignity onto the front lawn.

18. BENJAMIN'S BALLS

As we walk up and down the aisles of Adult Mart, I keep a close eye on Claire. She looks better after throwing up her dinner, but I'm still worried. I've never seen her sick before, unless you counted hangovers, and it puts me on edge. I hate that she's coming down with the flu and there is nothing I can do to make her feel better.

"This has burnt nut sac written all over it," Drew yells from the end of the aisle, interrupting me from my thoughts as he holds up a candle that doubles as massage oil when it's melted.

I reach for Claire's hand and give it a squeeze as we make our way down one aisle, glancing at things as we walk. I watch her carefully out of the corner of my eye, looking for warning signs on her face in case I need to rush her out of the store to defile more shrubbery.

"I'm fine, stop staring at me," she says without looking at me.

"Sorry, I'm just making sure you aren't going to throw up on the carpet. Out of all the fluids that are stained on this floor, I'm guessing vomit isn't one of them."

"Oh that's disgusting," she says with a laugh.

Seeing her smile puts me at ease a little bit. If she can still laugh, she isn't dying from some horrible, unnamed disease.

Claire suddenly stops and moves in front of me with a serious look on her face.

"You see?" she whispers conspiratorially. "This is why I have never set foot in one of these places," she states, looking over her shoulder and then back to me. "Look at that creepy, old guy over there in front of the 'Buy One, Get One Free' bin. He is about one 'Shaving Ryan's Privates' away from whipping his dick out in the middle of the store and throwing his goo at us like in 'Silence of the Lambs'," she complains.

She gives one last nervous look over her shoulder at him and lets go of my hand to go down a different aisle, clearly needing to distance herself from the guy who now has both of his hands in his baggy pants pockets and is jerking them at an alarming speed. The guy obviously hadn't read the sign hanging above the movies that said, "Please do not jerk off in our store. Thank you!" There is even a smiley face on the sign. It's oddly disturbing, yet comforting all at the same time.

I turn to follow Claire, stopping at a random display and grabbing the first bottle I see and read the back of it to see what it does. I read a few words when the sound of Claire's whispering brings my head up. I see her talking animatedly to Jenny a few feet away, most likely sharing her views about the DVD section and its inhabitants. I stand there for a few minutes just watching her when she suddenly throws her head back and laughs. It's one of those deep, full belly laughs that is impossible to stifle and it gives me goose bumps hearing it. It feels like someone punched me in the stomach and my heart starts pounding faster.

I love her so fucking much.

This isn't a revelation, but all of a sudden in the middle of Adult Mart I feel like nothing else matters but the fact that I love Claire. She is my dream come true, my life, and my everything. Does it really matter if I plan the best proposal in the world and spend weeks trying to come up with just the right words? She isn't the type of girl who cares about that stuff and I know it. I want everything to be outlandish because it's what I think is expected, not because it's what I think will be perfect for her. Asking her to be my wife and to grow old with me – that's what matters, not the amount of money I spend renting a jumbotron, or the meetings I have with the manager of a restaurant, or the stupid three-page speech I memorize. Waking up every morning next to this woman and tucking my son into bed every night is all that I care about. Claire and Gavin are my whole world, and I don't want to wait one more second to ask her to make it official in the eyes of God and everyone we know.

Spur of the moment. Isn't that the way you were supposed to do these fucking things anyway?

I swallow the knot that forms in my throat, suddenly nervous that the moment is here. The one I have been planning for and rehearsing – it's here and it's right fucking now.

I tear my gaze away from Claire for a moment and glance around me. Porn, dildos of all shapes, sizes and colors, and a shelf full of anal lube.

Jesus, does that say cinnamon-flavored anal lube? I don't even want to think about a situation that requires flavored anal lube. I must be insane that I am actually contemplating this right now.

I stand there with my hands sweating, heart pounding, and a bottle of Lickity Stiff Arousing Cream clutched to my chest.

Fuck it.

I take a deep breath, my decision made. With determination, I walk over to where Claire is still chatting with Jenny. She turns to face me just as I reach her and takes the bottle I'm holding out of my hand to read its contents.

"Lickity Stiff Arousing Cream? I'm pretty sure you don't need this," Claire says with a laugh.

She turns around to place it back on a shelf, and I take a deep breath for good measure, reach into my pocket, and wrap my fingers around the velvet box that I still carry around with me just in case. With Claire's back to me, I pull out the box and start to kneel.

"Holy shit!"

The exclamation interrupts my descent to the floor, and I pause with both of my knees slightly bent, looking like I'm getting ready to take off sprinting in a race. Claire turns around just as a hand clamps around my bicep and dragged me backwards.

"Liz, what are you doing?" Claire asks.

"Just need to talk to Carter for a second. Need a guy's opinion about porn, no worries!"

I stumble and shove the ring box back in my pocket as I try to turn around and keep up with Liz. Despite my protests, she continues to hold onto my arm and walk faster.

"Liz! What the fuck?! I was kind of in the middle of something," I complain as we get further away from Claire who stares at us with confusion on her face.

"Oh I know what the fuck you were in the middle of, dumbass!" Liz whispers loudly.

She finally stops when we are on the opposite side of the store from Claire and turns to face me.

"You're proposing to Claire?" she asks with her hands on her hips and a mixture of awe and anger on her face

"Well, I was *trying* to until I was rudely interrupted," I tell her, putting my hands on my hips and staring her down. She is small and feisty, but I have cocks on my side. Hundreds of them I can fling at her and then flee in the other direction when she attacks.

"You're proposing to Claire."

This time it's a statement rather than a question.

"Um, I think we already covered this. Let me guess, you think it's too soon. Or you're afraid I'm going to hurt her. Go ahead, give it to me. Wait, shit! Did she say something to you about not wanting to marry me? Fuck! She's been acting weird since your wedding, and I know she's talked a good game about not wanting to get married, but I figured it was just talk. What girl doesn't want to get married? Oh fuck, *Claire* is the type of girl who doesn't want to get married. Oh my God she doesn't want to marry me," I ramble as I pace back and forth in front of a display of chocolate body paint.

"Oh for fuck's sake, calm down, Nancy. I swear the two of you are the stupidest people I have ever met. You live together and you never talk. How is that fucking possible?" Liz asks in irritation.

"What are you talking about?"

168

Liz sighs. "YOU. ARE. STUPID," Liz repeats, enunciating each word and making up random hand gestures to go with each one so it looked like she was using sign language. Except I'm pretty sure the sign for "stupid" isn't a middle finger.

"I shouldn't be telling you this because Claire is my best friend and this seriously violates the best friend code of honor between girls, but we have a situation on our hands. I am willing to take a kick to the vagina for you when she finds out about this so you better clean out your ears and listen the fuck up!" she says with a poke to my chest with her finger. "Claire has been freaking out lately that *you* don't want to marry *her* because she has this idea in her head that you're a typical guy and the idea of marriage makes you want to puke, which could explain the purging she did in the landscaping out front. She doesn't have a porn fetish. She just didn't want you to know that ever since my wedding she's done nothing but think about marrying you, and she's scared to death it's going scare you away."

I stare at her with my mouth open, not sure which fact makes me more sad: Claire thinking I wouldn't want to marry her or Claire not really being addicted to porn. That is a problem I'm sure we can overcome together and without the tears or vomiting...unless that was the type of porn she was into, but I'm pretty sure we can get through that together as well. Maybe. But I guess that's a non-issue now.

"Okay, then why the fuck did you stop me? I was seconds away from easing all of her fears," I complain.

"Um, take a minute and look around, Romeo. Do you really want to propose to Claire in front of a display of cock rings?"

I glance around me and really take in my surroundings and think about what I'm doing.

"Years from now when she's retelling this story to your grand kids, do you really want her to say, 'Well kids, your grandfather popped the question right next to the anal beads and ball gags.'?" Liz says in a grandmotherly voice.

"I'm sorry, I don't get what the problem is here," Drew says as he suddenly appears next to Liz, licking a sucker shaped like a pair of tits.

"Go away, this is a secret," Liz tells him.

"Nice try, twat waffle. I heard the majority of what's going on. And I kind of want to take Carter here out back and rub my nuts on his head for not telling me he planned to propose to Claire in the happiest place on earth," Drew states, giving me a dirty look. Well, as dirty a look as he can with sugar boobs on a stick hanging out of his mouth.

"Isn't Disneyland the happiest place on earth?" Liz asks.

"It's like you don't even know me," Drew tells her.

"Look, this was a last minute decision. It's not like I planned to drop down on one knee in the middle of this place."

I look away from them to take another glimpse around me.

Why the fuck did I think this was a good idea? Claire would have killed me, murdered me where I stood. My obituary would read, "He died under a pile of pink and purple rubber cocks and double A batteries."

"I was caught up in the moment and just reacted," I tell them sheepishly.

Drew pats me on the back. "Awww, you got sentimental in a porn shop. Will you marry me instead?" he asked with a laugh.

I shut him up with a punch to his chest.

"Wait, if you didn't plan this, why are you carrying a ring around in your pocket?" Liz asks suspiciously.

"Uh, I, um, kind of carry it everywhere with me," I tell her, feeling beyond uncomfortable that I'm admitting this out loud. "I've had a few proposal plans go belly up the last few weeks. I've been wracking my brain trying to come up with the perfect plan and every time, something has gone wrong. I like to keep the ring in my pocket so I can reach in and touch the box. It gives me reassurance to keep trying."

Liz's bottom lip quivers and Drew stares at me blankly.

"Dude, you've been fingering that box in your pocket all this time? I thought you had crabs or something. I was going to let you borrow my cream," Drew says with a sad shake of his head. "That's pathetic. You have officially lost your man card. If you take it all back right now and tell me there's a hole in your pocket and you were just diddling yourself like the old guy over in aisle twelve, I'll forgive you."

Liz pinches the skin of his underarm, and Drew lets out a howl, rubbing the spot that is now turning red.

"Shut up, ass fuck. That is the most romantic thing I've ever heard," Liz says with a sniffle. "Let me see the ring."

I look behind me and find Claire perusing DVD's now that the guy playing pocket pool is gone. I slide the ring out of my pocket and quickly opened it for Liz to see.

"Holy shit, you went to Jared's," she whispers in awe.

"YES! Ha ha, vindication!" I shout with a fist pump.

Liz and Drew shush me and we all turn around to see if Claire has heard the commotion. I quickly snap the ring box closed and shove it back in my pocket to see that she is oblivious to the noise and is still neck deep in the clearance porn bin.

That is so hot.

Even if my grandmother walked in right now, I don't think I'd be able to get rid of my boner.

Sorry, Nana, my girlfriend is in a sex shop trying to pick out the perfect porno for us to watch later. Carter Junior isn't going anywhere for a while. Please pick girl-on-girl, please pick girl-on-girl.

"Oh for God's sakes, close your mouth, Carter, or you'll catch flies," Liz scolds, bringing my attention

171

back around. "And Drew, quit staring at Jenny's ass. You'll have plenty of time for that later."

"Actually, we've already done it three times today. I'm kind of spent," Drew replies with another lick to the sucker.

"First of all, that's disgusting and I would have slept a whole lot better tonight if you hadn't shared that, and second, when the fuck did you even find time to have sex three times? You were at my shop all day helping me unload inventory. You didn't even see Jenny until we got to the restaurant," Liz questions.

"*First of all*," Drew replies, mocking Liz. "You said 'load' and we need to acknowledge that. Heh, heh, load! And second, it was more like one point two times if you want to get technical. I had sex with the Jenny mold twice in the bathroom of your store, and I had sex with *Jenny* in the bathroom of the restaurant."

And there goes my boner.

"There are so many things wrong with that statement I think my brain just exploded. You're bleaching my bathroom tomorrow, asshat," Liz says angrily.

"Hey, what are you guys talking about?" Claire asks, coming up to the group.

"We're talking about how many times I spooged in Jenny today," Drew states proudly.

"Sorry I asked," Claire replies, turning right back around and walking away.

"Never, ever use that word again. Ever," Liz tells Drew once Claire is out of earshot. "Okay, Carter, I get where you were going tonight with the whole 'spur of the moment' thing and it's a nice touch. But you need a plan."

"Hey, Christopher proposed to Adriana without any kind of plan. He just walked into her mother's house and handed her the ring. Maybe he had the right idea," I told her indignantly.

"Who the hell are Christopher and Adriana?" she asks.

"Um, duh! From Sopranos," Drew replies.

172

"Come to think of it, though, it didn't really end all that well. He fucked everything in a skirt, snorted coke, shot up heroin, and had her killed. Plus, the reason he proposed was because he just beat the shit out of her," I reason.

"Gee, it's amazing you were able to come to the conclusion that basing your marriage proposal off of an HBO mob show isn't the best idea," Liz says with a roll of her eyes.

"Hey, as long as Claire doesn't go to the FBI and rat us out it could totally work," Drew states. "That's common sense right there. Bitches are snitches," Drew says, throwing down gang signs to emphasize his point.

"It's obvious I'm going to have to do this for you. Give me a few weeks and I'll have your problem solved," Liz assures me.

I'm not so sure having someone else plan my proposal to Claire is a good idea, but Liz *is* her best friend. Who better to help me out with this? Plus, it will alleviate some of the pressure I feel.

The three of us make our way back to the other side of the store where Claire and Jim are standing, staring slack jawed at Jenny.

"What should I do? He tells me to test them out, so I did. How was I supposed to know how far in to stick them?" she whines as we got to the group.

"What happened? What's going on?" I ask to no one in particular.

I notice Claire is looking a little green again, and I put my arm around her waist and pulled her in to my side.

"I bought some of those Benjamin Wa Balls, and I know you're supposed to try stuff out before you leave the store to make sure it works. Now I can't get them out," she complains.

It's not until that moment I notice she is standing with her legs slightly spread like she was getting ready to take a dump on the floor.

"Did she just say *Benjamin* Wa Balls?" I whisper to Jim standing next to me.

173

"Seriously? That's what you're concerned with? She stuck a product up her vagina before she left the store. And was planning on putting it back if she didn't like it," Jim whispers back in a horrified voice. "I should never have touched anything in here."

Jenny rocks back and forth from one foot to the other and shakes her hips a little in an effort to shake them loose I'm guessing.

"This Benjamin Wa guy should have come up with a better removal plan," Jenny states.

"Jesus, will you stop calling them that? They're BEN WA BALLS," Liz shouts. "And you're not supposed to test the products out IN the store. That's only for toys that require batteries and the clerk will put some batteries in to make sure the thing actually runs before you leave with it."

"How the hell was I supposed to know any of this? And I thought that was just a nickname for them and they shortened it to fit on the packaging. I was using the formal name," Jenny tells her as she continues to move her hips around in a giant circle like she's trying to hula hoop in slow motion.

We all just stand around staring at her while she does her weird mating ritual to get Benjamin's balls loose. It's like a train wreck we can't turn away from.

"I am never letting anyone use the bathroom in my shop. Ever," Liz says under her breath.

"Ooooh, I think I got one loose!" Jenny exclaims.

"I totally love you right now!" Drew tells her.

"I think I'm going to be sick," Claire states, throwing her hand over her mouth and running for the exit.

19. OOPS, I DID IT AGAIN!

After a week of being sick off and on, Carter forces me to go to the doctor. Other than throwing up a few times, I feel fine. I know he's making a big fuss over nothing. But regardless, I haven't been to my doctor for anything other than my yearly pap test since Gavin was born. He's a general practitioner so he is Gavin's doctor as well. With all the time I've spent in that office with my son and his check-ups, colds, shots, fevers, diaper rashes, and everything else under the sun, there is no need for me to go in there if it isn't absolutely necessary. I'm the type of person who doesn't go to the doctor unless I'm bleeding from the eyes or monkeys are flying out of my ass. I figure my heath and well being will be perfectly fine through osmosis just by walking into that place every couple of months with my son.

When I call my doctor and tell him my boyfriend is being mean and making me get a physical, his exact words are, "Claire, you know there's more to you than your vagina. I've scheduled you for tomorrow."

Whatever. What if my vagina *is* the best part? What do you have to say about that, Doctor Dick?

Actually, I really do love our doctor. I have never seen him wearing anything other than jeans and a t-shirt. He's very down-to-earth and Gavin loves him. Plus, if I'm going to let a guy stick his hands up my snatch once a year, he better make me feel comfortable if he isn't buying me dinner first.

I'm currently sitting on the exam table in a lovely ensemble of a paper shirt that opens in the front and a paper blanket the size of a newspaper that is supposed to fit around my ass. The room is a balmy fifty-two degrees, and I have been waiting forty-five minutes so far. Needless to say, I'm in a super mood by the time Dr. Williams finally shows up.

175

"Claire, how are you doing today?" he asks as he walks into the room with a nurse following close behind.

"Oh, I'm just super. Did you do something new with these gowns? They seem to have much more coverage," I say sarcastically.

"Ah, Claire, you always say the nicest things," he laughs as he takes a seat on his little stool with wheels and looks over my chart.

The nurse comes up next to me and takes my blood pressure and checks my pulse, reporting the numbers to Dr. Williams so he can notate them.

"Well, your BP is good and you don't have a fever. When was your last menstrual cycle?"

I count backward through the weeks in my head and then stop and count again.

"Well, it was...I remember it was a Tuesday because that's the day my supplies are delivered, and I was in the middle of signing for the white chocolate when I felt cramps," I ramble, trying not to panic.

One, two, three, four, carry the seven, multiply by eight...FUCK!

I glance over at the calendar hanging on the wall. This month shows a black and white cat with wide eyes and both of its paws covering its mouth as if to say 'Oops!'.

Fuck you, you stupid cat! I can't count with you staring at me like that. And if cats really could say "Oops" they'd do it when they shit on the SIDE of the litter box instead of in it.

I stare at the squares and the numbers on the calendar until they all start to blur together, either from eye strain or tears, I'm not sure which.

"First, how about we just have you scoot down to the end of the table and we'll check you out. You're due for your yearly exam next month anyway so we might as well get that taken care of," Dr. Williams says as he slides his chair closer to me while the nurse pulls out the extension at the end of the table and adjusts the stirrups for my feet.

I lie back and put my legs up in the air while the nurse slides a table over with the pap test kit already set up on top.

Right now, I wouldn't mind a little Drew humor to take my mind off of things. Something to the effect of, "How's that cunt scrape coming along?"

I squeeze my eyes shut while the doctor goes to work, sticking his hands where only one man has gone before.

"So, have you been watching the new Bachelorette? That chick is a train wreck!" Dr. Williams says with a laugh.

"Um..."

"Did you see when she got all trailer park on that one guy? Wagging her finger and shaking her head? You can take the girl out of the trailer park..." Dr. Williams trails off with another laugh as I hear the metal clink of the speculum.

"My daughter likes to watch that stupid show just to see the pretty dresses she's going to wear," he tells me as he continues working between my legs.

No really, it's perfectly fine to talk about reality television and YOUR KID while your fingers are all up in my business. How does this work when he's at home? Is it the exact opposite when he's sitting around the dinner table? "So did I tell you about this woman today? Her cooch hadn't been shaved in days. What a trainwreck! Can you pass the potatoes? I only treat her because she's got a pretty uterus. How did you do on your spelling test, Cindy Lou?

Dr. Williams finishes digging to China, slides back and slips off his rubber gloves while he stands.

The nurse takes my arm and helps me sit up. I try to situate the paper shirt and skirt thing to cover myself back up but it seems like the fucking thing shrunk. I give up and just keep my legs as tightly together as I can. It doesn't seem appropriate to flash the goods to the doctor now that the exam was over. It would be like walking up to your dentist in the grocery store and showing him your teeth. There is a time and a place for everything.

177

"So? Is everything okay? What's next?" I ask, hoping since he hasn't said much during the exam, aside from television gossip, that all is good and I'm worrying for nothing.

"Well, we'll order up some blood work, and I'll see you back here in four weeks," he said with a smile as he wrote something else on my chart. "Congratulations, you're pregnant!"

~

Did you know The Dollar Store sells pregnancy tests? It's true. And even though all these stupid dollar stores should change their names to "The Dollar Store – Everything Isn't Really a Dollar, We Just Like to Fuck With You", pregnancy tests are in fact one of the few things there that actually only cost one dollar. Which begs me to ask the question why the hell did I get a dirty look from the cashier when I asked for all thirty-seven tests? Like that's never happened before? They are pregnancy tests for ONE DOLLAR, people. Gavin gets one dollar for doing chores around the house every once in a while. Even HE can afford to buy a pregnancy test. Why a four-and-a-half-year-old would need to buy a pregnancy test is beyond me, but these are the facts.

Arguing with the cashier and telling her I hope she slams her ginormous tits into the drawer of the cash register probably isn't my finest moment, but it keeps my mind off of the fact that I might be pregnant.

Yes, I said *might*. I have just finished peeing on the twenty-third test and Dr. Williams had told me I was pregnant when he fondled my uterus, but he could have been wrong. Doctors get things wrong all the time. They remove a kidney when they mean to remove a gallbladder, and they forget to take clamps and shit out of someone before they sew them up. He could definitely be wrong about my uterus. How many uteri does he stroke on a daily basis? Maybe he's just off his game. Maybe he hadn't even been touching my uterus but had his hand around my spleen. But that would probably mean he was up to his elbows in my vagina. It had been uncomfortable, but not elbows-deep uncomfortable.

I stand at the sink in the bathroom and stare at the pregnancy test in my hand, waiting for the five minutes to be up so I can gouge out my eyes when I see another positive result. When the timer on my cell phone beeps with the new tone ("SWEET MOTHER FUCKING JESUS IT'S TIME!") I downloaded just for this purpose, I glance down and try not to cry.

An hour later, Carter and Gavin come home from the store and find me curled up in the fetal position on the floor of the bathroom, surrounded by used pregnancy tests, instructions, and ripped open boxes.

"Mommy, where did you get all these magic wands?!" Gavin asks excitedly as he runs into the bathroom.

He picks up one of the tests and pretends like he's Harry Potter, aiming the test at random objects around the small bathroom yelling, "I curse you with my magic wand, punk toilet paper!"

I don't even lift my head from the cold tiles; they feel too good on my tear-stained cheeks to move. I watch him with my eyes and wonder briefly if I'm a bad mother for letting him play with something that I peed on. That just starts another crying jag when I realize I will be a bad mother to *two* kids now. I have a vision of the future where both of my children are sitting in a tub of pee while I'm comatose on the floor.

Carter walks to the doorway and takes one look at me and the litter on the floor and jumps into action.

"Hey, Gavin, how about you put down that wand and go get the bubbles we just bought. I'll even let you blow them in your room."

"Sweet! This wand smells funny anyway, and it's making my hand wet," Gavin states as he drops it on the floor and runs from the room.

"You should probably tell him to wash his hands," I mumble from the floor.

"Eh, he's going to be playing with bubbles, which are like soap, so it will all even out," Carter replies as he steps into the room and sits down on the floor next to me.

I sit up, pushing tests and boxes out of my way so I can cross my legs and sit Indian style across from him with our knees touching.

"So, how was your day?" Carter asks gently as he reaches over and brushes my hair out of my eyes.

I sniffle and look around at the mess.

"Oh you know, the usual. I worked, ran some errands, some guy put his hands up my chimichanga, complimented my uterus, and I got into a fight with a clerk at The Dollar Store."

"Was it because practically nothing in that store is a dollar?" he asks.

"Oh my God, right? What the fuck is up with that? I don't go into a store called The Dollar Store to buy a five dollar toy. Someone needs to school these people on proper advertising," I complain.

A few seconds of silence lapse, and I knew Carter was waiting for me to mention the huge "I'm pregnant" elephant in the room. Fuck that elephant! He can just sit there in the corner eating peanuts and shitting on the tile while giving me looks of disgust.

You're the one shitting on the floor, elephant, don't give me that look.

Carter spreads his legs out on either side of me, reaches over and grabs onto both of my ankles, unwinds my legs, and pulls me across the floor to him. He re-hooks my ankles together behind his back and puts his hands on either side of my face, forcing me to look him in the eyes.

"Say it," he whispers. "I missed out on this the first time. I want to hear you say it."

My throat is so tight I'm positive I won't even be able to take another breath, and he wants me to talk?

"Please?" he pleads softly.

He smiles at me and I can see his eyes start to fill with tears. I want to tell him so many things, but

I'm too overcome with emotion and frankly, a little bit of puke. Two words are about all I can muster.

"I'm pregnant," I whisper back with a sniffle.

"You're pregnant?" he asks with a huge smile.

Um, duh? What the fuck do you THINK all this is about? Oh my God, what is wrong with me? I'm sorry! I love you!

"Are you not happy about being pregnant?" he asks, showing the first sign of worry since he stepped into the room.

"I figured YOU wouldn't be happy. You're totally screwed now. If you decide you don't like me, I've got you for eighteen years. I'm your baby mama times two. That's triflin', yo."

Carter laughs and wrapped his arms around my waist so he could pull me up against him.

"Stop trying to quote Kanye. You're not a golddigger, and there's no question whose kids they are," he tells me as he cups my cheek with one hand and rubs it softly with his thumb.

"That's what you think. Sperm from the floor of the sex toy shop might have jumped off of the carpet and up into my vagina. No telling who this one belongs to."

He stares at me for a few minutes before kissing the tip of my nose.

"I know you're freaking out. It's okay. Just talk to me. Whatever you're feeling, I want to know. And I am perfectly fine with this. In fact, I am EXTATIC with this. There is absolutely nothing that could ruin my good mood about this news," he affirms.

There cannot be a more perfect man in the world than him. Fact.

"Really? Because I'm pretty sure we conceived this child the night I ate that pot cookie. I'm eighty-four percent positive our child is going to be born a pot head. It's going to come out with dreadlocks and wearing a Bob Marley onesie. Its first word will probably be, 'Whaaaaaazzzzzzzzuuuuup'. It's never, ever going to sleep through the night because it's always going to have the munchies."

181

Carter chuckles and tightens his hold on me. I wrapped my arms around his neck and rest my chin on his shoulder.

"If that's the case, we'll just have to make sure we have plenty of Cheetos on hand at all times and some Grateful Dead music to play in the nursery," he states.

I sigh and turn my head so I can rest my cheek on his shoulder and burrow into the side of his neck.

"It's going to be fine. I promise you. I love you and I'm not going anywhere. This is the best news you could have ever given me. Nothing could make me happier right now."

Gavin suddenly comes bursting through the doorway.

"Dad, woke up dis morning, got myself a gun' is on!" he says excitedly. "And my wiener feels funny again. It won't stop being tall."

"Oh my God. I take that back. THIS is the happiest moment of my life. My son just got a boner for Sopranos," Carter whispers.

"Like father like son," I deadpan.

Carter pulls me up from the floor of the bathroom and tells me to leave the mess and that he'd clean it up later. He tells me I'm not allowed to do anything else for the rest of the day but lie on the couch and let him wait on me. He always knows exactly what to say to make me feel better, and he takes such good care of me. I'm an idiot for being disappointed that he doesn't immediately ask me to marry him. He loves me and he's happy we're going to have a baby. I can't help but wonder though why he hadn't asked. He obviously isn't in shock like I am so there has to be another reason. As I curl up on the couch with my head on Carter's lap, I try to ignore the pain in my heart at the thought that maybe he doesn't think I was marriage material.

20. DID NOT FINISH

Three months later

"So what you're telling me is you wanted him to drop down on one knee and ask you to marry him in the bathroom?" my mother asks.

I roll my eyes and reached for another balloon to blow up. My mother has offered to help me set everything up for Gavin's fifth birthday party the next day. We are having it at the shop after hours. I let Gavin invite a few of his friends from preschool and think having a party in a candy store will be fun for them. As soon as my mother walks in the door of the shop she can tell I'm not myself. I blame my mood swings and crying jags the last few months on pregnancy hormones, but she knows better. The number of times we've talked on the phone, I gloss over what's wrong. Now that she can see me in person, I can't hide anything from her.

"Don't roll your eyes at me, chickadee. I'm just trying to make sure I understand this correctly," she says as she hangs a "Happy Birthday" banner on the wall. "You thought it would be romantic and beautiful if, once he found out you were pregnant, proposed immediately. So you wanted him to propose out of guilt and obligation for knocking you up instead of out of love."

Well when you say it that way...

"No! I mean...I don't know. I just would have liked for the effort to have been made. Maybe even a comment about us getting married or getting engaged at some point in the future. The fact that he hasn't said one word about it in three months just sucks," I tell her. "Every day I keep waiting for him to bring it up and every day that goes by and he doesn't, I get more upset. What if he doesn't think I would make a good wife? I know he loves me, but maybe he's not IN love with me. The kind of love that makes you want to do everything in your power to ensure you spend the rest of your life with that one special person. Maybe I'm not that special person for him."

Jesus. Talk about depressing. How does anyone even stand to be around me lately? I'm a disgusting, emotional, needy chick. No wonder Carter doesn't want me.

"It makes sense I guess. Look at all the years I spent hating the idea of marriage. I thought it was pointless and could only end in disaster. Karma is biting me in the ass."

My mom walks over to me and pulls me into her arms, my growing stomach acting as a stopper to keep us from getting too close.

"Baby, any fool can see that Carter is IN love with you. Have you ever paid attention to that boy when you walk into a room? His whole face lights up. And he's constantly touching you in some way. A brush of his hand on your cheek, wrapping his arms around your waist, kissing your shoulder...he does whatever he can to be close and connected to you," she says, pulling away so she can look at me. "And don't give me that bullshit story about you hating the idea of marriage."

I give her a pointed look and laughed.

"Are you kidding me? You and Dad were married five times total. FIVE TIMES! When you know your parents crashed and burned so many times, it's kind of obvious that you're going to have the same luck," I tell her.

"Oh, sweetie, you are a jackass. I love you, but you are dumber than a one legged duck in an ass kicking contest when pigs fly," she tells me.

"Am I supposed to know what the fuck that means? You either told me this was impossible or called me a pig."

My mom reaches up and wipes a tear off of my cheek I don't even know is there.

"Marriage was never for me. I knew that early on but I chose to ignore it. I never dreamed of having a family or a house with a white picket fence and being a soccer mom. But then I had you and I knew I needed to

184

try. It just didn't work for me. But your father? He is definitely a marrying man, and he is a wonderful husband. The problem was never him. It was the losers he married," she says with a smile. "You may have always been afraid to try because of how you grew up and what you believed, but that doesn't mean it's who you are. You have more of your father in you than you know. You are already a better mother than I ever was, and I guarantee that when Carter *does* pop the question, you will be an amazing wife."

For the first time in my twenty-five years, my mother actually says something that made sense and gave me pause. And not the "What the fuck is she saying?" pause.

I had put up a wall all my life to protect myself. If I pretended like I didn't really want the American dream of a husband and kids, then eventually I would believe it and no one would be able to hurt me. Until Liz and Jim's wedding, I didn't realize just how much I wanted that wall to crack. Now that it had though, I was right where I never wanted to be - scared, confused and upset. I knew I needed to get my emotions under control and stop acting like a crazy person. I needed to man up and talk to Carter. I could feel the distance between us growing every day that I continued to lie to him and explained away my detachment and rocky emotions by saying they were all just because of the pregnancy. I had acted like a big baby all these months when all of it might have been fixed by one little conversation.

After Gavin's party, I will make sure that we sat down and talked.

"What about Carter's family? Are his parents still trying to recover from ceiling fan baseball?" my mom asks with a laugh, changing the subject to something a little less depressing.

"They've been okay. His mom actually sent me a big box of brand new baby clothes and a few blankets. His grandmother is the one I'm most surprised about. She really should want to kill me but she sent me

185

something too, and I found out she actually has a sense of humor."

"Oh? What was it?" my mom asks.

"A onesie that said 'Too cute to play with your ugly ass kid'."

~

"Why the hell are those bitches over there giving me a dirty look?" Liz asks as she stares down five mothers who have accompanied their sons to Gavin's party.

"I'm guessing it's because the woman who brought her husband just noticed that he's been staring at your boobs that are spilling out of your shirt," I tell her as I finish cutting the cake and placing it on paper plates.

"Oh give me a break. One look at that guy and you can tell he's wound up so tight that if I blew him a kiss he'd probably bust a nut. None of those women look like they ever have sex unless it's to procreate," she complains.

"They probably only do it in the missionary position with the lights off," I add.

"I bet they think doggy style is a type of line dance," Liz says with a laugh, blowing the husband a kiss.

I smack her hand and give her the evil eye.

"Will you cut it out? I have to be around these mothers all the time at Gavin's school. Play nice," I warn her.

"Look!" she says excitedly. "That poor guy just adjusted his junk. He totally came in his pants."

So far the party has been a success. The kids are yelling and running all over the shop now that they are hopped up on sugar. I had thought having them frost their own cookies would be fun until they forgot about the cookies and started shoveling frosting into their mouths by the handful. Having Drew wrap up a bag of Pixy Stix and a twenty ounce can of Mountain Dew as Gavin's present doesn't help matters either. He tears into the present and has half the candy and all the Mountain Dew gone before I even notice. By the time I get a hold of him, he looks like he's been snorting coke off of hookers. His eyes are bloodshot, his hair is a mess, and he has white powder all around his mouth. When I see Drew whisper in his ear right before Gavin runs up to me and yells, "I have tiger blood running through my veins!" I know it's time to take the kid-crack away from him

And of course I get nothing but dirty looks from the world's most perfect mothers. They can't just drop their kids off and come back like normal parents who foam at the mouth when they find out they'll get a few hours of peace and quiet and make their kids jump out of the moving vehicle at the curb before peeling off to get a massage or go to the bar. Oh no, they have to stand in the corner in their perfect little clique, judging me with their pastel sweater sets, linen pants, and string of pearls. Drew has already told one of them he has a much better pearl necklace he can give her later that night, hence the huddling in the corner. I think they really thought he was going to whip his dick out at a children's party and jerk off on one of their necks. Actually, this is Drew I'm talking about. There's a distinct possibility he might do it.

They spend the whole day looking put-out that they had to be here. They turn their noses up at my store-bought decorations and one even says, "Oh, so you didn't do centerpieces and table favors? And I heard you say this wasn't catered? That's a shame." Um, correct me if I'm wrong, but this is a party for a FIVE YEAR OLD. Not a fucking Bar Mitzvah. I'm not decoupaging anything, using a glue gun, or whittling an ice sculpture, and I sure as hell am not serving lobster and filet. I feed them pizza and hot dogs and fill goodie bags with Play Doh and bubbles. Where I come from, that's how you celebrate a toddler's birthday. I hold my tongue, though, because I don't want to be *that woman* who got into a cat fight at her kid's birthday party.

I'm tired, cranky, and on edge as it is because I haven't talked to Carter yet. He had worked last night and we drove separately to the party so he could sleep. If another one of those uppity bitches says anything else to me, I'm not going to be responsible for my actions.

Liz grabs two plates of cake and leaves to take one over to Jim and antagonize the lone father whose wife probably threatened his manhood if he didn't come with her to the party.

She probably told him he wouldn't get missionary birthday sex this year where he could rub on top of her for thirty seconds while she was fully clothed. Poor guy.

"Hey, how are you feeling?" Carter asks as he comes up next to me and helps put forks on all the plates with a slice of cake on them. We've only said a few words to each other in passing since he got here. Both of us have been running around making sure everyone was happy and the party was a success. He had looked a little horrified at first when he got here, having never experienced a little boy's birthday party before, but he quickly jumped right in, grabbed a can of Silly String and began screaming and running around with the kids.

"I'm okay. Just tired," I tell him. I want to throw my arms around him and tell him I'm sorry for being such a bitch lately, but I know it will make me cry and I'm not about to do that in front of all these people. He seems nervous standing here with me and it makes me sad that I've done this to him. Instead of wrapping his arms around me and making a joke like he normally would, he keeps his distance, probably afraid I will snap at him or burst into tears like I've done for three months.

I am the biggest bitch in the entire world.

I turn to face him, knowing I need to say something to clear the air even if it's just to tell him I love him, when one of the she-wolves stalked over and interrupts us.

"Excuse me, but I think you should know that your son just said a bad word," she informs me haughtily with her hands on her hips.

Son of a bitch. This is so not what I need right now.

"I'm sorry. What did he say?" I ask.

I wonder if she's too appalled to say whatever the word is out loud. She's probably going to spell the word for me, and I'm going to have no choice but to point and laugh at her. F-U-C-K, A-S-S, S-H-I-T…what's it gonna be? Hopefully she knows how to spell bad words or this is going to be a whole new level of awesome.

Drew comes up to us and the woman looks at his shirt that says "Have you seen my perfect man ass?" and huffs in irritation.

"What's the dillio, folks?" he asks, taking a bite out of a cookie and spitting crumbs as he talks.

"I was just telling Claire that Gavin said a bad word in front of my son," she explains again.

"We're really sorry," Carter reiterates.

"So what did he say? Cocksucker, thundercunt, fuckholes, ballsactitties? Drew asks in all seriousness.

Under normal circumstances I would have probably smacked him in the arm for this, but the shock on Mother Theresa's face across from me is satisfaction enough. I put my hand over my mouth to cover up my giggle.

She sputters and gasps a few times before she finally replies angrily. "For your information, he said the word c-r-a-p."

The three of us stand there looking at her funny.

"Well? Aren't you going to do something about that?" she asks when no one says or does anything.

"I'm sorry, did you just spell the word *crap*?" Drew asks in confusion.

"Yes, that's the word Gavin said," she tells him.

Drew starts laughing. Loud, gut busting laughs.

"Oh my God! You totally had me going there for a minute," Drew tells her between laughs. "I really thought G-man was going to be in trouble."

189

The other mothers must have heard the commotion and walk over to join our small group.

"I should have known you wouldn't do anything about it. I mean, it's obvious you don't know the first thing about being a good parent. The parenting skills you have shown are appalling. Letting your child run amok, talking like a veteran trucker or a sailor. Real people do not talk this way to each other. The amount of times I've heard the word v-a-g-i-n-a alone is shocking. If this whole display was a story I was reading, it would be a disappointing 'did not finish' for me."

Oh no she DIDN'T!

I stand there for a few minutes with my mouth hanging open in shock while the other Stepford mothers get on the "you're a shitty parent" bandwagon and nod their agreements. These women are real pieces of work. I mean, I would totally talk about you behind your back, but I'd never be that mean and bitchy to your face or say something to hurt your feelings.

Until now.

You bitches messed with the wrong pregnant woman.

"Oh, I'm sorry. I didn't realize you cornered the market on perfect parenting. Isn't that your son sitting on the floor over there eating his boogers and naming his farts? Real genius you've got on your hands there. And you," I say, turning to one of the other ones. "Your kid told me when he got here that he wasn't allowed to eat processed sugar, white flower, red dye number five, or watch Spongebob because it was too violent. Isn't he the one sitting on the chair by the door rocking back and forth chanting 'I hate humans'? My child may be mouthy, and he may say inappropriate things from time to time, but I am a damn good mother. I just found out today my son scored higher on his kindergarten testing than all of your little fuckwits put together. He may watch Spongebob, he may eat sugar, and he may pick up on phrases the adults around him say, but I can guarantee you that when he's older, you won't find a human head in his freezer like little Johnny over there who's been banging his head against the glass for an hour because he's in shock from having a piece of cake for the first time in his life. And for your information, real people *do* actually talk like this. Really cool people who have awesome friends don't have giant sticks up their asses like you obviously do."

Carter leans close to my ear. "Gavin scored that well on his testing?"

"I know, total shocker for me too. He obviously doesn't get his brains from us," I whisper to him.

I turned back and realized all of the women have dispersed from our fun little pow-pow, grabbed their kids, and scurried out the door without another word.

"Oh and by the way, we should probably look into some new preschools," I state.

21. I SWALLOWED A PENNY!

"What do you mean you aren't going to do it?" Liz screeches. "Carter, we've been planning this for weeks. You HAVE to do it."

Liz and I are in the kitchen of the shop doing dishes while Claire is out front with everyone else taking down decorations.

I know Liz means well, but I just can't do what she wants me to.

"Liz, this just doesn't feel right. It was a great idea before she got pregnant, but I just can't do this now. Claire hasn't been herself since she found out she was pregnant. No matter how many times I try and tell her that everything will be fine, I don't think she believes me. If you hadn't told me what you did about her being afraid I didn't want to marry her, I would have thought she was cheating on me," I say.

"Um, dude. She's got your sperm inside of her. That would be gross. And if you were so worried, why the hell haven't you proposed yet?" Liz questions.

"Because you told me you'd cut off my dick if I did!" I argue.

"Okay, that may have been a little extreme. But I knew she would think you were doing it just because she was pregnant. I figured if you waited a while and I kept telling her she was an idiot, everything would work out and you could propose without her thinking bad things."

I sigh and crossed her arms in front of me. "I can't wait any longer, Liz. I know we planned on me doing this next month on the anniversary of when we first met, but I can't put this off one more day. There is this huge wedge between us right now and I have a feeling it's all because of this. I should have just said something to her months ago. To hell with the surprise."

"Fine. Have it your way. But I swear to God if you just walk up to her and hand her the ring, I won't

192

cut your dick off, I'll just cut one ball off. You'll be forever known as Uniball Carter," she warns.

We stare at each other for a few minutes, her eyes narrowing with each second that passed.

"You don't have a plan, do you?" she finally asks.

I should tell her to move away from the knives.

"Um, not exactly. I mean, I know what I want to say. I just don't have all of the details yet," I admit.

"Well, I'd help you, but I kind of want to punch you in the face. You're on your own with this one," she tells me, throwing the towel she dried the dishes with onto the counter. "Now I'm going to have to tell everyone that the plan is off. It was the one time I was looking forward to wearing a shirt that Drew picked out."

I feel bad that Liz has spent all this time helping me plan something amazing for Claire. At the time, we had both agreed it would be awesome if our friends were there to see the proposal, and Drew of course wanted everyone to wear matching shirts that Claire would see right after I proposed. They *were* pretty great shirts and that is the one thing I will regret not doing, but I know this is the right decision.

"So does that mean no Gavin either?" she asks as she leans her hip against the counter.

"No, no Gavin. As cute as it would be for him to be the one to hand her the ring, I need to do this by myself. It was just the two of us the day I met her, and I want it to be just the two of us when I ask her to spend the rest of her life with me," I explain.

Liz let out a great big sigh and finally concedes.

"Alright, I get it. Your ball is safe from my wrath. But just so you know, I'm going to hold this against you for a long time," she tells me with a pat on my back.

"I wouldn't expect any less. I just need you to do one more little favor for me."

"What now? My first born, a pint of blood, one of my limbs? I've already given so much!" she wails in mock horror.

193

"Oh quit being such a drama queen. I already told you I appreciated your help so cut the shit out. I just need you to get Claire out of the store for about an hour. Can you do that?" I ask.

"No problem. I have this raging yeast infection from having too much sex in our hot tub. I'll tell Claire she needs to come to the pharmacy with me and help me pick out the right YEAST INFECTION cream," she says, putting the emphasis on the words that make my skin crawl.

"Liz, too much information," I say with a grimace.

"But it's really yeasty. I could make a loaf of bread with this shit."

"OH MY GOD! Cut it out. I'm going to puke," I tell her.

Liz laughs as she walks around the counter to go out front and talk to Claire.

"Payback is a bitch. And YEAST INFECTIONS really itch," she yells back to me with another laugh.

I try to block the last few minutes of conversation from my mind as I get to work planning how this will go down. Claire sticks her head into the kitchen doorway a little while later to tell me she was running to the store with Liz. I can't help but laugh a little when she whispers, "She's got an issue. And she needs my help. It's...an issue. I'll be back soon."

Right after she disappears from sight, Liz pops her head in to give me one more parting shot.

"Say 'bacterial vaginosis is delicious'. SAY IT!"

~

I honestly don't remember a time when I've been this nervous. I would have taken a minute to run to the bathroom and throw up the contents of my stomach, but I just heard the bell over the door of the shop ring and knew Claire was back.

I take my place at one end of the kitchen island and wait.

Claire walks through the doorway seconds later and stops, a look of confusion on her face as she takes in the sight before her.

"Um, why are there red Solo cups all over the counter?" she asks.

"I thought we could take a trip down memory lane and play a little beer pong," I tell her with a grin.

She walks further into the room.

"Nice sentiment and all but I don't I want our child to be born a pot head *and* a drunk."

I laugh and pick up the empty milk jug for her to see.

"Technically, this is milk pong."

She laughs when she gets to the other end of the island and glances into the cup closest to her.

"Ahhh gotcha. If I remember correctly, I kicked your ass the last time we played," she says with a smile.

"Oh I don't think so. I'm pretty sure all of the ass kicking was done by me. You sucked at beer pong."

"Lies! Not only were Liz and I the lap dance champions in our dorm, we were also beer pong champions," she told me with a satisfied smirk.

"Wait, what?"

She laughs again and shakes her head at me. "I know I told you this story."

"No, I'm pretty sure I would remember every part of a story that involved you and lap dancing," I argue.

"Liz and I used to do lap dances on each other for free beers at the college bars. I was a little bendier then so I was usually the one on top," she says nonchalantly.

Claire, bendy, girl lap dances...my penis exploded. That JUST happened.

"Promise me I will get to see this someday very soon," I tell her.

"Yeah, okay. Because pregnant chick lap dances are so hot." She chuckles.

"I don't think you understand how serious I am right now, Claire. This is right up there with meeting God and winning the lottery."

Seeing her happy and smiling confirms my decision to do this right now, this exact way. If only I could get the image of Claire grinding on another woman out of my head.

Damn you, penis, you aren't in charge tonight! Take a break, go back to sleep, nothing to see here.

"As much as it pains me to say this, the lap dance can wait, but you're going to have to prove to me right now that you've still got it in beer pong. The ping pong balls are right in front of you. Put your ball where your mouth is."

She raises her eyebrow at me.

"Hmmm, that didn't come out right. But I kind of like it," I tell her with a shrug.

She picks up one of the balls and lines up her shot. It bounces off the rim of the first cup and lands in one behind it.

"Yeah, that's what I thought," she taunts as I remove the ball from the cup and drink the milk.

I set the empty cup to the side, pick up my own ball and take aim while trying to keep my hand from shaking. I know I need to make as many shots as I can for this to work out the way I want it to. I toss the ball and it sinks right in the cup closest to her. I let out a huge sigh as she removes the ball and picked up the cup.

"Lucky shot," she tells me before downing the milk.

"I love you more than I ever thought was possible," I tell her softly as she sets the cup down. She cocks her head to the side and smiles at me.

I pick up another ball and quickly throw it before she could say anything back to me. It sinks into another cup right in front of her. As she picks up the cup to drink it, I speak again.

"I love you because you make me laugh and you make me want to be a better man."

196

I already have another ball in my hand and throw it into the air before she even finishes the last cup of milk. She stares at me wide-eyed as the ball plops into the next cup in line and she hesitates before picking it up. I wait until the cup is by her mouth before I continue.

"I love you because every day you amaze me."

A lone tear escapes from her eye as I throw another ball right into a cup. I've never played this well in my life. I guess it's only fitting since this is the only game where I'm playing *for* my life.

She picks that cup up and sniffles before taking a drink.

"I love you because you are the best mother in the entire world."

One more to go. And this was the one that counts. I aim and watch the ball sail in an arc toward the last cup on her side of the counter. I hold my breath until it drops right where it needs to go. I walk around the counter until I'm next to her and wait for her to finish the last cup of milk.

A surprised gasp sounds from her when she tips the cup back and something bumps against her lip. As she pulls the cup away from her mouth and looks into the bottom of it, I get down on one knee.

With shaking hands, she reaches her fingers into the cup and pulls out the diamond ring I have been carrying in my pocket for months. She turns to look at me and gasps again when she sees where I am.

"The first time we did this, every time one of us sunk a shot we would tell each other a fact about ourselves. I remember you told me your favorite color was pink and that you watched the movie 'Girls Just Want to Have Fun' once a year because it made you nostalgic for the time when Sarah Jessica Parker didn't look like a troll."

Claire laughs through the tears that are now falling freely.

"This time, I needed you to know every fact about why I love you. I wanted to marry you the first time I saw you again. I wanted to get down on my knees and beg you to never leave me. And I should have done it. I should never have waited this long. There is no one else in this world I could imagine spending my life with. I want to teach inappropriate things to our children with you forever. Claire Donna Morgan, will you please, *please* marry me and love me for the rest of your life?"

She leans over and throws her arms around me, holding me tight as she sobs out the one word I have waited forever to hear from her.

"Yes!"

I pull out of her arms long enough to take the ring from her hand and slip it on her finger. Our happy moment is interrupted seconds later by Gavin running into the kitchen.

"Mom, guess what? I swallowed a penny!" he announces.

Claire and I pull away from each other and turn to see all of our friends and Claire's father standing in the doorway wearing the shirts Drew had picked out that say, "I played beer pong and all I got was this lousy t-shirt, knocked up, and a fiancé".

"Sorry, Carter, I couldn't resist the shirts. And really, they're still appropriate considering how you proposed," Liz says with a smile.

"Wait, I'm sorry. But did Gavin just say he swallowed a penny?" Claire asks, wiping the tears off of her cheeks.

"Oh, yeah. Well, we *think* he swallowed a penny. We're not quite sure," Drew explains. "He wanted some candy so Liz dumped out her purse on the floor because she knew she had a bunch of Tic Tacs at the bottom. He started scooping things up and shoving them in his mouth before we saw what he was doing. According to him, he swallowed a penny. But kids are liars."

Gavin stomps his foot. "YOU'RE A LIAR YOU BIG FAT TURKEY!"

"I am not fat. I'm muscular. Get your facts straight," Drew argues.

"Okay, can someone please tell me if my kid really swallowed a penny?" Claire asks loudly, putting a halt to the arguing.

"Well, I Googled 'kids swallowing pennies' and you'd be surprised how many hits I got," Liz says. "Anyway, as long as the penny was made before 1982, he'll be fine."

Claire and I stare at her for a few minutes before Claire explodes.

"What the fuck?!"

"Awwwwww, Mom," Gavin scolds as he pointed at her.

"I'm sorry, what the f-u-c-k does t-h-a-t mean and w-h-a-t do we do n-o-w?"

She has officially turned into one of the Stepford mothers, spelling words she doesn't even need to spell because she is so freaked out. She is not going to be happy about this.

"It's fine, Claire. I used my metal detector on him and the penny wasn't there," George stated.

"You're kidding me, right? You know there's this fancy thing called a hospital you can go to, don't you?" she asks.

"I walked uphill both ways in a snow storm with no shoes just to get to school when I was his age, and I ate metal shavings for fun. A little copper isn't going to hurt him," George argues.

"Unless the penny was made after 1982 because then it's made with enough zinc to melt his esophagus," Drew said matter-of-factly. "I'm pretty sure that would have happened by now though, so he's probably good."

Claire bends down next to Gavin and pulls him into her arms.

"Sweetie, how do you feel? Is your tummy okay?" she asks him.

"My tummy is good. Papa said I need to drop a deuce and check it for money. I can poop money!" he says excitedly.

"I wish I could poop money," Drew complains.

I bend down next to Claire and Gavin, gathering both of them in my arms.

199

"Just so you know, we're totally eloping," I tell her.

"Oh thank God," she replied.

22. HUMP, HUMP, HUMP

"So you really like it?" Carter asks for the hundredth time.

We are finally in bed relaxing after the long day, and I can't stop staring at my ring.

"I think I like it more than you."

Carter laughs. "Very funny."

"Oh, I'm totally serious. I've been thinking all this time that you just didn't want to marry me and here you were carrying a ring around in your pocket. I kind of want to whittle my toothbrush into a shiv and stick it in your eye," I tell him seriously.

He rolled over onto his side and rested his hand on my stomach.

"I'm sorry. I should have done it the day I bought the ring. I just wanted it to be perfect and then we found out you were pregnant and I know how your mind works. You would have never believed I was doing it for the right reasons if I did it right when we found out," he says as he gently rubs his palm in a circle on my protruding belly.

"I know, you're right. My mother said the same thing," I tell him, placing my hand on top of his and pushing it down towards the bottom of my stomach where I usually feel the teeny tiny kicking of little feet. To me it feels like bubbles popping, and I'm not sure if he would be able to feel it yet but it doesn't hurt to try.

"Rachel actually said something that made sense?" he asks in surprise.

"Yeah, it shocked me too," I say, turning my head on the pillow so I can see his face. "I should have just talked to you. Obviously I suck at the whole communication thing. I'm much better at suffering in silence."

Carter scoots closer and moves his hand out from under mine, sliding it up the front of my body until it rests on my cheek.

201

"I think we both have a long ways to go in the communication department. We'll get there though," he assures me.

"Did I tell you that when all this doubt crept into my mind I told Liz about it and she suggested that I give you a prostate massage?"

"Oh my God, stop. Don't say any more. Jim actually told me about the night she did that to him and it was horrifying. Please don't say any more," he warns.

"I don't know, you might like it," I tease.

"*Hey, I don't even let anybody wag their finger in my FACE,*" Carter says in a Brooklyn accent.

"Seriously? A Sopranos quote now?"

"Um, yes. There is a Sopranos quote for every occasion. Hence, the reason for its awesomeness. Respect The Sopranos," Carter tells me seriously.

I roll over onto my side toward him and slide my leg up and over Carter's hip, running my fingers through his hair.

"I think we should celebrate this momentous occasion by me sticking my penis in you," he says with a smile.

"You're lucky you gave me jewelry today or I might have punched you for that."

Carter pulls me closer and brings his lips to mine. Just like always, his kisses make me forget about everything. The softness of his lips and the smooth glide of his tongue against mine remind me of just how long it has been since we've had sex. With our crazy schedules and my attitude problem, it's been a while and I am more than starved for him. His arms wrap around me and his hands slide down to my ass, cupping it and pulling me in against his hardness. I shift my hips against him and let out a groan.

"Wait, hold on. Shit," he mutters, breaking off the kiss.

I pull my head back and shoot him a questioning look.'

"What? What's wrong?"

Is his penis broken? Oh dear God please don't let it be broken. I NEED IT TO LIVE.

"I have to pee. Hold that thought," he says, pulling out of my arms and scrambling off of the bed.

I roll over onto my back and stare up at the ceiling. A few minutes later I still hadn't heard the toilet flush.

"Hey, are you okay in there?" I yell.

"SHHHHHHH! NO TALKING!" he yells back.

What the fuck?

"What do you mean no talking? What the hell is going on?"

I hear a few expletives coming from the bathroom, and I raise myself up on my elbows so I can look at the closed bathroom door.

"I can't pee!" he finally yells back.

"What do you mean you can't pee?"

Holy shit, it really IS broken. I knew I should have used it more these past few months. Son of a bitch! It broke from non-use.

"Seriously, you need to stop talking. You're making it worse."

"What the hell are you talking about? How am I making it worse?" I argue.

The door to the bathroom finally opens and he stands there with his hands on his hips and a tent in the front of his boxers.

"Because, your voice turns me on and I can't get rid of my fucking boner! I would never say this to you under normal circumstances but this is an emergency. So shut the hell up for a minute so I can pee!"

With that he goes back in the bathroom and slams the door closed behind him.

Well, at least it still works.

~

"Oh it was awesome once we got past Carter's freak out," I tell Liz the next day on the phone. "He was convinced the baby could see his penis and would

203

either get jealous or have nightmares for the rest of its life about a penis monster trying to eat its face. Then he wanted to try and find a condom because he though his sperm might drown the baby. I actually had to bring my laptop into bed and show him that his penis would need to be two feet long for it to get anywhere near the baby."

Carter is working the day shift today and I'm spending the late afternoon taking down wallpaper in the room that will eventually be the nursery. I'd been at it for a few hours and was exhausted. I had taken a break to call Liz and report to her about how the rest of our evening went. Since she had constantly berated me the last few months about how often we WEREN'T having sex, I felt she deserved an update. After a few minutes we end the call and I decide to take a trip up to the local corner store to get one of my current pregnancy cravings: a black cherry slush. So far I've had one every single day since the day I found out. They are delicious and refreshing and the only place that sells the black cherry ones is the place right around the corner from our house.

I pack Gavin in the car and head down the street. Once inside the store, I make a beeline for the slush machine in the back, dragging Gavin along with me. I get to the machine and stopped in my tracks, staring at the sign that's taped to the front.

"Out of order? What do you mean, out of order?" I say out loud.

"It means it don't work," Gavin says.

"I know that's what it means. But it's a slush machine. It turns water into ice and you add cherry syrup to it. How hard can it be for a machine to do that?"

I see that the machine is still plugged in so I let go of Gavin's hand, grab onto it, and start jiggling it back and forth.

The power light doesn't come on so I start pressing all of the buttons over and over. When that doesn't work, I start smacking the side of the machine with the palm of my hand.

"Mom, you're gonna break it," Gavin warns.

"Stupid piece of shit machine. All you have to do is make ice you worthless pile of horse shit!" I say to it, completely ignoring Gavin.

Oh my God I need this slush. I need it like I need air to breathe. Why the fuck won't it just work!

At this point I'm pretty sure my brain has left my body. I continue to physically assault the machine, hitting it with my fists and cursing at it like it's a person who can fight back.

"Nothing to say for yourself, asshole? You can't even TRY to work? You lazy piece of shit. Get off your ass and make me a slush!"

People are starting to stare. I can feel their eyes on me as I rape the slush machine with my hands. I pull cords, I stick my finger in holes, and I remove the entire front cover, exposing all of the inner workings.

"Ma'am, I'm going to have to ask you to step away from the slush machine," a man in a corner store uniform tells me.

"Why the hell isn't your machine working? You need to fix the machine," I tell him, standing there with the cover of it in my hands like it's a shield.

"I'm sorry but there's a part that isn't working. We had to order a new machine and it won't be in until next week," he explains, prying the cover out of my hand and setting it aside.

"Next week? NEXT WEEK? What are people supposed to do for slushes if they have to wait a week?" I ask.

"God doesn't want you to have a slush," Gavin tells me.

I look down at him questioningly.

"God is king of the world and he says you don't need a slush. Can I get some ice cream?" he asks.

"God doesn't know. HE DOESN'T KNOW," I complain.

I'm pretty sure I'm having an out-of-body experience. I can see myself acting like a complete douchebag, but there is nothing I can do about it. I'm like a junkie that needs a fix. My hands are shaking, my head hurts, and I'm about two seconds away from selling my kid and my shoes for another hit of black cherry slush.

I take Gavin's hand, walk calmly out of the store, and drive home.

As soon as we get in the house I grab the phone and call Carter. He picks up on the first ring and all I can do is sob hysterically.

"OH MY GOD, CLAIRE?! What's going on? Is everything okay? Is it the baby? Did Gavin get hurt?" he shouts.

"The slush machine was broken!" I wail.

Dead silence on the other end.

"I'm sorry, what?" he asks.

"Did I stutter? The slush machine was broken. I couldn't get my slush. I need a fucking slush!" I cry.

"Wait a minute, this is all because of a slush?" he questions.

Oh my God, it's he doesn't know anything about me. How can I marry someone who doesn't understand me?

"I thought something serious happened," he says irritably.

"Something serious DID happen! Are you even listening to what I'm saying?"

Carter sighs and I try to calm myself by NOT thinking about how much I want a slush. Instead, I think about how I want to stick my fist up Carter's ass and give him a prostate massage with my fist.

"I'm getting off of work in a few minutes. My parents should be there in about an hour."

Oh shit. The future in-laws are in town for a visit. *Thank God I didn't get arrested at the corner store. That would have been awkward.*

"I'll bring you a slush on my way home," he promises.

"Black cherry?"

"Yes, black cherry," he confirms.

"I love you! See you soon!"

~

Carter's parents show up right on time. Thankfully I finish my big gulp slush by then and can carry on a normal, non bat shit crazy conversation. Madelyn walks through the door first and tells us all to come in the living room and close our eyes because she has a surprise for us. A few seconds later, Charles says, "Okay, open them!"

Gavin and Carter let out excited yells and I groan.

"A puppy! A puppy! You got me a puppy! I can hug it and squeeze it and ride it like a bike and give it haircuts!" he shouts excitedly as he gets down on the floor.

The puppy, if you can call it that, is almost the same size as Gavin, and it looks like a polar bear.

"Is it even legal to own one of those?" I question. The more I look at the thing, the more I wonder if they really did just bring us an endangered animal that will grow to be nine-hundred pounds. Do you have any idea how big of a shit a nine-hundred pound animal takes?

"This is a pure bread Great Pyrenees," Madelyn tells me, expecting me to be impressed.

I'm not.

"Wow, this is awesome. Thank you guys so much. You know I've always wanted one of these," Carter tells them.

I look at him in shock. He's always wanted a horse for a pet? This thing is going to be bigger than our car.

"How exciting. We get to house-train a dog AND a new baby. Can they both be taught to shit outside? Or should we put a diaper on the dog? Pick one, because we're not doing both," I whisper to Carter as he pets the dog, and his parents take a seat on the couch.

"Don't worry. It will be fine," Carter whispers back as he stands up and lets Gavin run around the room with the dog playfully following behind him.

"The first time he shits in my shoes I'm going to rub *your* nose in it," I threaten.

"I have all of the American Kennel Club paperwork for you out in the car as well as the authenticity papers from the breeder," Madelyn tells us.

Super. Our dog has more class than we do.

"What's his name?" Carter asks.

"Reginald Phillip III," Charles answers.

"Oh, that's getting changed immediately," I mutter.

"I want to call him Bud," Gavin states as he runs around us in circles with the dog right on his heels.

"That's a good name," Carter tells him.

"I know. I'm naming him after the daddy juice you drink."

"How about we wait a little bit before deciding on a name," Carter tells him.

"Reginald Phillip, get down!" Madelyn scolds.

We turn around to see the dog mounted up on Gavin's back with his paws on his shoulders. Gavin just keeps moving and laughing. It looks like a freaky version of the locomotion dance.

"Ha ha. What's he doing?! This is fun!" Gavin laughs.

"Oh my God, he's humping our kid," I mutter, smacking Carter on the arm so he will do something.

Carter runs over and pulls the dog off of Gavin by its collar.

"Heeeey, why'd you do that? We were having fun," Gavin complains.

"Uh, he was trying to pee on you," Carter tells him.

I look at him like he's insane and he just shrugs. "What? I panicked. I can't tell him what humping means," he says quietly.

Gavin lets out another excited yell and once again, we find the dog hugging onto his shoulders and thrusting his hips behind him.

"Hump, hump, hump. I'm gonna pee on you! Hump, hump, hump!" Gavin chants as the two hop around the room and Carter tries to separate them again.

"Obviously you'll want to have him neutered as soon as possible," Madelyn states with a straight face.

Gee, you think? The dog is trying to breed with my son.

"All aboard the choo-choo train, all aboard the choo-choo train, WOOT WOOT!" Gavin sings with the dog happily enjoying his caboose position.

"Carter, get me the hose."

23. SCITTLY SCAT-SCAT

Five months later.

"Last chance to change your mind. You're sure this is what you want to do," Carter asks as he starts the car and backs out of the driveway.

"I swear to God if you ask me that one more time, I'm going to straight up murder your ass. It's like you *want* me to wreck my vagina," I tell him.

Today is the big day. The one I have been equally dreading and looking forward to: my scheduled c-section. We are on our way to the hospital now so I can get checked in. Carter has been questioning my decision to have a repeat c-section since the day the doctor asked me about it six months ago.

"It's not that. I just want to make sure you don't regret never having the experience of actual childbirth. I've heard that some women who have c-sections get really depressed because they didn't get to know the joy of pushing their child out," Carter explains.

"I'm sorry, who are these women you spoke to? Did you make a trip to a mental hospital recently? What woman in her right mind would regret that her vagina didn't turn into a gaping, bloody wound with bodily fluids pouring out of it and a baby clawing its way out, sometimes ripping and tearing until her vagina and asshole are just one big disgusting abyss?" I ask.

"Forget I said anything. I just want you to be happy," Carter states diplomatically.

"Some women take a dump on the birthing table when they are pushing their kid out. Do you really think that's an experience *you* want to have?" I question. "I've heard the nurses make quick work of cleaning it up before anyone notices, but you'll notice. Believe me. How can you NOT notice the room suddenly smelling of fecal matter?"

"Stop, please stop," Carter begs.

"I am very happy with my decision. And you should be happy that six weeks from now, banging me won't feel like waving a stick in a cave or dipping your pinkie into the Grand Canyon."

"Okay, I get it," Carter says as he pulls into the hospital parking lot.

"Thrusting a pencil into a fireplace...shoving a piece of straw into a barn door," I add.

"Why am I getting turned on right now?" Carter asks as he finds a parking space and we get out of the car.

"Are you into scat play? You're not going to make me poop on you at some point are you? Tell me now so I can give you this ring back."

Carter ignores me as we get into the elevator and make our way up to Labor and Delivery. But I will not be ignored. Oh no, I will not be ignored.

"Scittly scat-scat, do bop dee scat!" I sing as we walk up to the nurse's station and hand them my admitting forms.

The nurse gives me a funny look so I feel it's only right to explain to her my song choice.

"My fiancé wants to me to poop on him," I tell her. "Scat-scat, dee didily bop!"

"Oh Jesus, I'm sorry. I don't know what has gotten into her this morning," he explains, shooting me a dirty look.

"It's perfectly fine." The nurse laughs. "It's just nerves. Believe me, I've heard worse from other women checking in." she told us.

What nerves? I'm not nervous. I've done this before. Piece of cake.

"We'll just get you settled into a room down by the O.R., start an I.V. of fluids, and have you fill out your registration forms. The doctor will come in and talk to you as well as the anesthesiologist. I'll stop by after that to give you a dose of Bicitra to drink. It's a small little cup of liquid that will help if you happen to get nauseous during the procedure. After that, it's go time!" she says excitedly.

What the fuck have I done?! Turn back NOW!

"I changed my mind. Maybe I do want a black hole for a vagina. How bad could it be? I wouldn't

211

need to carry a purse anymore. I could just shove things up my twat. 'Oh, you need a pen? Hold on, let me check in my vagina. What's that you say? Do I have a flashlight? Let me stick my hand up my vag and find out.' Let's go home. We could do a home birth in the bathtub. It might be a tight squeeze but I bet we could both fit in there," I ramble to Carter.

"Can we get some morphine to go?" I ask the nurse.

She just chuckles as she shows us to the room and gets busy typing things into the computer while Carter pushes on my shoulders to get me to sit on the bed.

"Everything is going to be fine. Take a deep breath," Carter tells me.

"They are going to cut open my stomach and pull a human out, Carter," I whine.

"I know, babe. I'm nervous too. But you've done this before, and you know exactly what to expect. You know what it's going to feel like, you know how long it's going to take, and you know what the end result will be...finally being able to see our baby," he says with a smile as he leans down and kisses the top of my head. "At last we can find out if we'll have a Carmela or a Tony."

"Oh I don't think so. We've already had this discussion and we are NOT naming this kid after some ass munchers on the Sopranos. Get that thought out of your head right now," I tell him.

"You are such a killer of dreams, you know that?" he complains.

~

"Just remember, Carter, when the baby is out, we'll have you come down here to the foot of the operating table so you can take pictures and watch your little one get cleaned off, measured, and weighed. But don't forget, whatever you do, don't look at Claire," the doctor warns.

"What the hell is he talking about," Carter whispers, leaning down by my ear.

I'm strapped to the operating table with my arms stretched out in a T on either side of me. A huge, blue drape is attached to two I.V. poles on both sides of the table and placed strategically so I can't see past my boobs. When I had my c-section with Gavin, I wondered what the big deal was of putting this drape up. Maybe I wanted to see what was going on down there and make sure they didn't screw up. Then a few months later, I had watched a c-section on the medical channel and I almost threw up. NOT something you ever want to see being done to yourself, mark my words.

"I'm pretty sure they just don't want you to look over at me with my guts hanging out all over the place and freak out," I tell Carter.

"Okay, Claire, you're going to feel a lot of tugging now as we get the baby out," the doctor tells me.

I definitely remember this part from the first time. Not painful, but really fucking weird. Like someone is grabbing onto your stomach skin with both hands and yanking it all over the place. The fact that I know there's a doctor shoulder-deep inside my stomach right now is what's more painful.

Carter sits on a stool right by my head next to the anesthesiologist and keeps smoothing a few stray pieces of hair out of my eyes that have escaped from my hospital cap. He continues to ask me how I'm doing and kisses my forehead every few seconds, telling me how much he loves me and how proud he is of me. He is so strong, and I am once again reminded of how lucky I am to have this amazing man in my life.

"Okay, Carter, get your camera ready. When I say the word, you can stand up and aim your camera over the top of the sheet to take a picture," the doctor says.

"Try not to get my internal organs in the picture. They don't photograph well," I tell Carter.

213

He fiddles with the digital camera and gets it ready. I look back at his upside down face and see him smiling from ear to ear. Everything about this past year from the good and the bad to the ugly is all worth it because of this moment right here. Carter had missed out on seeing the birth of Gavin and that fact still makes me sad. But he is here now and I hope that seeing his next child born will ease a little of that ache for him.

"The baby's out! And it's a girl!" the doctor exclaims. "Get your picture, Dad!"

Carter jumps up and holds the camera above his head, quickly snapping a picture before sitting right back down and raining kisses all over my face while I cry.

"A girl? Are you sure? Is she okay?" I ask through my tears.

The next sound we hear is the wail of a healthy set of baby lungs.

Carter laughs through his own tears and continues kissing away mine.

"Oh, baby, you did it! I'm so proud of you. We have a girl!"

The anesthesiologist makes some adjustments to my I.V. now that the baby is out, and I momentarily wonder if would be okay for me to just start chanting "Morphine, morphine, morphine!" really loudly.

"Come on back, Dad, and see your little girl," one of the nurses says.

Carter gives me one more kiss on the cheek before he gets up and begins to walk around the I.V. pole to make his way to the end of the operating table.

"Carter, don't forget, don't look at my—"

"OH JESUS CHRIST! IS THAT HER INTESTINES?? WHAT THE FUCK IS THAT? OH MY GOD!"

I hear the sounds of tennis shoes squeaking on the floor as nurses most likely race to Carter's side to get him away from the horror show.

"Oh fuck me, did I just step over a tube of blood that is draining out of her and into a bucket? What the fuck is that for?"

214

When you have a c-section, there's not much you can do but lie there and listen to the commotion going on around you. It's not like you could be all, "Hey, Doc, can you give me a minute? I need to get up and check on my fiancé and make sure he doesn't puke on our new baby." I had been given a spinal before this thing which meant I was numb from the neck down. I'm not any good to anyone right now.

"They told you not to look!" I shout to Carter.

"That is the number one thing you should never say to anyone! Of course if you tell me not to look, I'm going to look," Carter says as his voice gets closer and closer. Oh my God, Claire, I think I saw your spleen sitting on your chest."

The next thing I know, Carter is right next to me holding a tiny, perfectly wrapped bundle of baby. She looks like a little burrito wrapped tight in her white, blue, and pink hospital blanket and pink baby hat on her head.

Carter brings her right up to me and sets her down on the pillow next to my head so I can kiss her cheek.

"Oh my God, she's perfect," I cry as I stare at her sleeping face.

"Well, kind of perfect. I think she has Elephantitis of the vagina though," Carter tells me quietly.

I laugh and reach an arm over to stroke her soft, pink cheek.

"That's normal. All babies have enlarged genitalia when they're born," one of the nurses says as she walks past us to get something from a drawer against the wall.

"Oh yeah, you should have seen the size of Gavin's balls when he was born. Jesus. He could have fit a small country into those things," I say.

"Hey, maybe that's just the way he was supposed to be born. You know, taking after his father and all," Carter says as he leans down and kisses our little girl's cheek before kissing mine.

215

"Okay, Dad, if you want to go with your little girl down the hall to the nursery you can help give her her first bath and give the good news to your family members," the doctor says. "We'll have Claire down in recovery in about forty-five minutes. We just need to sew her up."

A nurse comes and scoops up our little girl and places her in the bassinet with a sign on the end that reads "Sophia Elizabeth Ellis, 7lbs, 10oz."

I refuse a Sopranos name, but I concede by letting Carter pick an Italian name.

"I love you so much," Carter tells me, cupping his hand on my cheek and leaning over my head to kiss my lips upside down.

I turn my head to the side and watched the love of my life walk behind the bassinet that holds our new daughter.

When they are gone, I close my eyes and try to enjoy the morphine coursing through my veins and count all of the amazing blessings I have been given. Unfortunately, I keep losing count. As the doctor sews me up, he and the nurses count out loud and it's very distracting. I had asked during Gavin's c-section what the hell they were doing and I was told that they have to count all of the instruments and sponges to make sure none are left behind. At the time, I thought it would be funny to start saying random numbers out loud to see if it would break their concentration. Two, seven, one, fifteen, thirty-five. But then I had realized it wasn't as funny if it was *my* body cavity they were losing these things in. It's hilarious when it's someone else, not so much if I have to go back to the hospital six months later because there's a pair of scissors stuck to my kidney or I'm shitting out sponges.

I block out the incessant drone of counting and think about just how perfect my life is now. I can't wait for Gavin to meet his new little sister, and I am actually excited to show her off to Carter's parents. It's a toss-up though on whether or not I'm so happy because I know the next four days will be spent getting waited on hand and foot with morphine and vicodin to

216

cheer me up should I ever feel like slitting my own wrists.

The man I love more than anything wants to marry me, we have an amazing little boy who keeps us on our toes, a new, healthy baby girl, and the best family and friends. Okay, maybe not the best. Tolerable. Life is good. Nothing can take this feeling away right now unless the anesthesiologist turns off my morphine drip. I'll just take away his manhood if that happens. I'm sure the doctor can find an extra scalpel in my intestines for me.

"Wow, would you take a look at that?" I hear the doctor say.

"Oh my," one of the nurses replies.

"Uh, what's going on?" I ask.

"Can someone get me a camera?"

Okay, that's not something you need to hear when your stomach is cut open and you're strapped to a table.

Someone take this mother fucking sheet down. I don't give a rat's ass if I can see right through my stomach and out my vagina. I'll even help you stuff shit back in.

I can hear some whispering, which makes me a little uncomfortable. I mean, what could they possibly be whispering about? Is there another baby in there no one knew about? Have they found an extra stomach? Maybe I'm supposed to be a twin and I ate her. Have they found my twin sister? Is she looking at them right now like, "What the fuck, people? Get me the hell out of here. I'm twenty-five and I'm the size of a fist. Do I look like I'm comfortable?"

I have always wanted a sister. I can carry her around in my purse like Paris Hilton carries her dog. I can perch her up on my shoulder and she can be like the good angel telling me what decisions I should make.

What if she's mean though? Twenty-five years is a long time to be in someone's stomach. Jesus himself would probably even drop a few F bombs about that nonsense. She might sit on my shoulder and just shout insults at everyone.

217

"You're tired? Fuck you. I've used a uterus as a pillow for twenty five years."

"I've taken dumps bigger than your penis. And I had to do it in a stomach with a baby looking at me."

"You're so ugly I wouldn't even let you fuck my tiny, fossilized punany."

Mmmmm, this morphine is delicious. Like pot cookies and vodka but without all the weird side effects like hallucinations and crazy talk. I love morphine. It's so pretty.

"Oh, no worries," the doctor finally answers. "Your uterus is just in a weird shape right now. We have a wall of pictures in my office of people's organs and it's kind of like when you look up at the sky and guess what a cloud looks like. Except we do it in my office with pictures of afterbirth and uteruses. I'm just going to take a quick Polaroid and then finish sewing you up."

Nope, that's not at all weird. Doc, can you supersize that morphine for me?

"So, what does it look like?" I asked.

I don't really want to know the answer to this do I? The drugs say yes but the brain says no.

"It actually looks like a face. And it's smiling at us."

OH MY GOD, SISSY! I'm coming for you sissy!

"HOLY SHIT!"

EPILOGUE

"I think this will be the first bubble bath I've taken alone in three years," I tell Carter as he sets a glass of wine on the edge of the tub and bends down for a kiss.

I wrap a wet hand around the back of his neck and hold his face to mine. He sweeps his tongue through my mouth and I taste the wine he had taken a sip of before he gave the glass to me. Even after all these years I can never get enough of kissing this man. It's our third wedding anniversary and a few months after Sophie's third birthday. For the past three years, we've spent our anniversary the same way – at home with the kids. And I wouldn't have it any other way. We don't need a fancy restaurant or a night out with friends. We have all we need right here.

Our wedding had been just a simple ceremony on the beach with our family and friends. After all the drama about getting engaged, both of us realized we didn't care about anything but becoming husband and wife. It didn't matter where it happened, just as long as it *did* happen. For an early wedding gift that year, Carter had given me all four seasons of "My Fair Wedding" and a box of porn. He still holds out hope my porn addiction would become a reality.

Carter slides his hand down into the water and lets it rest on the inside of my thigh. As the kiss became more intense, his hand inches further and further down. I groan into his kiss as his fingers graze between my legs and make goose bumps break out on my skin.

"Happy anniversary, Mrs. Ellis," Carter whispers.

The wet, smoothness of his fingers slide through my slit and I thrust against his hand as he slowly pushes one finger deep inside me.

A commotion from outside the bathroom door ceases all activity and we pause, my lips brushing against Carter's and his hand resting between my legs.

"What was that?" I whisper.

"It's nothing. The kids are in Gavin's room playing. I gave them a piggy bank full of pennies to count," Carter reassures me as he begins kissing his way down my damp neck and goes back to gliding his finger in and out of me.

"Ohhhhh fuck," I moan, tilting my head back until it rests against the tile wall. "You should probably check on them. The penny thing worked when Gavin was four. I don't think it's going to work now. He's almost nine, knows how to use the internet and is tall enough to reach the matches and lighter fluid in the laundry room."

A crash and a yell sound down the hall and I sit up quickly, splashing water over the side of the tub, forcing Carter to fall back onto the floor on his ass.

"Shit. I'll go check it out," he says with a sigh as he stands up and opens the bathroom door. "We'll continue this after I've duct taped them to the wall."

He closes the door behind him and I lean back into the warm, soapy water with a smile on my face.

The past few years have been hectic, but I wouldn't change them for the world. A year after Sophia was born, we had moved into a new home. The small, ranch house was perfect when it was just the three of us, but once you had a baby, it came with a lot of shit. We had quickly outgrown that house and moved into a two-story colonial a few streets away from Liz and Jim.

Business at Seduction and Snacks is still booming. I've added more items to my menu so people can have breakfast or lunch there, and I've hired five additional people to the staff. Liz and Jim had just gave birth to their second baby girl last month and Jenny and Drew are planning a weekend wedding in Vegas in a few months. I'm pretty sure that plan includes being married by Elvis and spending time in a lot of strip clubs. Jenny had finally found another job in marketing but still works for me on the side. She refuses to take any money from me though so I pay her in chocolate. Drew still begs me to pay her in sexual favors and is sadly disappointed every time I refuse.

Gavin is now eight and a half years old and getting ready to start third grade and our baby Sophie is growing up entirely too fast. She'll be going to preschool this year and I want to sob every time I think about it. Gavin is an amazing big brother and has spent the past three years teaching his little sister everything he can about tormenting us. The other day, Sophie had come into our bedroom and announced she had a song she wanted to sing us. It had gone a little something like this, "I have a vagina, vagina, vagina. I love my vagina, vagina, vagina." So far I haven't been able to convince her that this song should never be sung at the top of her lungs in the middle of the cereal aisle of the grocery store.

My father had married his long-time girlfriend Sue a few months ago in a small ceremony in his backyard. Gavin, Sophia, and Sue's granddaughter Sarah made up the wedding party. Sarah and Sophia were the same age and Gavin escorted both of them down the aisle. And by escorted, I meant kept the two girls separated since they kept trying to smack each other with their flower girl baskets as they walked until they eventually took Gavin down with them in a big pile of flailing arms, legs, screaming, and crying. Carter and I ran down the aisle and tried to break up the fight but Jesus, those girls were strong. Carter got kicked in the nuts and dropped down to his knees, and I got scratched in the face. Regardless, it was a beautiful ceremony and my mother, in her usual fashion, took control of Tee Time at the small reception. Jenny almost became "that person" who puked on the dance floor, but a cousin of my father's dragged her into the bathroom and showed her a trick where you drink straight from the faucet and then make yourself burp three times. Jenny had wound up making out with her as a thank you, and Drew passed out cold when he witnessed it.

221

I sink down further into the water and let out a big sigh. We've all come a long way since that frat party nine years ago. Carter and I still play a round or two of beer pong on the anniversary of when he asked me to marry him though. There are some traditions that you just can't put a stop to. Beer pong is how we started and beer pong is how we will end. I have a picture of us on our death beds years from now with a hospital table set up between us as we argue over who sucks more. And then that happy picture is ruined by Drew ambling in with a walker shouting, "Jenny can still suck a golf ball through a garden hose and she gums my cock like a champ since she misplaced her false teeth!"

I can't wait to see what the future will hold for us. We've had our ups and our downs, and we've had our fair share of struggles over the years, but we have proven that we can get through anything. Our beast of a dog, aptly named Gigantor, recently became a big brother himself when Carter's parents dropped off a cat for Sophie. Of course it had come with special hoity-toity cat papers that said it would walk around with a stick up its ass and demand to eat off of our good china. Since I nipped the whole Sopranos thing in the bud when we named our daughter, Carter had adamantly insisted we name the cat Meadow, after Tony Soprano's daughter. Aside from that, Carter has proven a thousand times over what a wonderful father he is. I had been a little nervous at first how he would handle having a little girl, but he was amazing and he was very protective of his daughter. So much so that my father had bought him a shirt that said "Sure you can date my daughter. In a completely unrelated topic, have you seen my shotgun?"

And now my wonderful husband is off taking care of the kids so I can relax in a bubble bath alone without someone coming in to pee, brush their teeth, or ask me why monkeys have nipples. Nothing can ruin this perfect moment or my happy mood thinking about the future.

"Hold still for a second. I need to get it in the right spot," I hear Gavin say softly on the other side of the door.

"What's going on out there? Where's daddy?" I shout out to him.

"He poopin', Mommy!" Sophie yells back.

Thanks for letting me know.

"You guys be good out there, okay? Mommy will be done in a minute," I shout to them as I picked up my wine glass from the edge of the tub and took a healthy sip.

I close my eyes and let the tension ease from my body until a few minutes later, words are loudly whispered by Gavin that you never want to hear on the other side of the door when you're taking a bath.

"Okay, the clothes basket is in the ready position at the edge. All systems go. Sophie, hold on tight. And don't let go of the cat."

The End

Made in the USA
San Bernardino, CA
03 November 2012